MADISON REEVES

PROJECT BAD ASS

BREAKING OUT OF YOUR COMFORT ZONE TO TRANSFORM FROM AVERAGE TO EXTRAORDINARY

Published by Mandala Tree Press
www.mandalatreepress.com

Paperback ISBN: 9781954801240
Hardcover ISBN: 9781954801257
eBook ISBN: 9781954801264

BUS025000 BUSINESS & ECONOMICS / Entrepreneurship
SEL027000 SELF-HELP / Personal Growth / Success
YAN010000 YOUNG ADULT NONFICTION / Business & Economics

Cover design by Kelly Carter
Edited by Justin Greer
Typeset by Kaitlin Barwick

www.projectbadassbook.com

THIS BOOK IS DEDICATED TO ALL OF THOSE
WHO INSPIRED WHAT IS CONTAINED INSIDE,
INCLUDING THOSE WHO MAY NEVER READ IT.

CONTENTS

PART 3:
GETTING OUT OF THE BUCKET | 69

PART 4:
RUNNING TOWARD
YOUR EXTRAORDINARY LIFE | 87

FOREWORD

BY JEFF CHRISTIANS

THE FIRST TIME I MET MADISON, SHE CALLED ME AN ASSHOLE!
We were at a real estate convention in Dallas eating dinner
with a large group, and she was a few seats down. We were all
talking about real estate, growth, and learning. She looked at
me and said, "Jeff, in all the time I have spent in this real estate
brokerage, I don't think you've ever once looked me in the eye.
You're an asshole!"

Now, I'm usually busy, so I hadn't intentionally been
ignoring her. We have our own team office next to the main
office. At that time, we had a team of about five agents and
four full-time administrative employees doing over a million a
year in commissions, and Madison was very new to real estate.

I was taken aback by her comment, so I just looked at her
and said, "You need to get results to get on my radar!" I think
the table was a bit in shock, but it's important to know where
to use your time most effectively.

Well, that must have lit a fire because a few months later,
she became a business partner on our team. She sold almost
forty homes in just eight months on our team at only nineteen

years old! Our team is on track to do over two million in commissions this year with her help!

Madison is a true entrepreneur as she also owns a wedding planning business that is run by someone else. She has learned leverage at a high level already. This girl crushes it and gets results! Madison is a forward-thinking visionary badass that takes action and gets massive results. Now we are going around the country speaking together and teaching real estate agents how to sell fifty-plus homes and take ten weeks off.

In this book, you will learn how Madison restructured her mindset from scarcity to complete abundance. She will walk you through how to deal with your limited belief and past trauma. She uses an amazing analogy about how humans are like crabs in buckets and why your friends and family may be the ones stopping you from success. Finding your "Big Why" can be such a challenge, but this book will walk you through that as well. Madison gives you the roadmap and actionable items in each chapter. No matter what age you are or what stage in life you are at, you will have some great action items to take your life to the next level! Also, don't forget to add Madison to Instagram because she posts awesome motivational content! Now go crush it!

JEFF CHRISTIANS
CEO of Christians Team, Inc

AUTHOR'S NOTE

As I tell my stories and the stories of others throughout my book, I have changed names and identifying details to protect those people and their personal experiences. Thank you for supporting me on this journey.

Enjoy! xx

INTRODUCTION

I'VE ALWAYS WONDERED WHY I STOOD OUT FROM THE OTHER kids—why my desires were different. Even as an adult, it's hard to relate to other people my age or to friends and family. For as long as I can remember, I have felt like this, perhaps because I've had this vision for myself, this grand life that I want to live. Even though I grew up poor, with little education and even less knowledge about how to reach my grand vision, I still wanted it. Growing up, I didn't realize that there was an entire world of like-minded people and resources out there that would eventually help me achieve this extraordinary life that I so badly wanted.

I grew up in a town of 5,500 people, graduating with a class of less than 100. In this community, it was not uncommon to get married young, have a few kids, and, just a handful of years after graduating, be back on those bleachers, watching your kids play soccer and basketball from the sidelines. There are kids (now parents) from my graduating class doing exactly that. There is absolutely nothing wrong with that, but personally, I have never wanted anything to do with that lifestyle. In fact, I couldn't understand why seemingly no one else was questioning why things were the way they were. It felt as though I was the only one who believed this typical, mundane, white-picket-fence lifestyle wasn't the be-all or end-all. I felt alone because my vision of this grand life seemed appealing only to me. As I look back, I realize that I was not the only one questioning the societal status quo. Chances are, if you're reading this, you are second guessing it all too—and I want you to know you aren't alone.

While growing up, I truly wanted nothing to do with this "normal" lifestyle, so I rebelled. But not in the typical way you might see in a high school kid who starts partying and staying out too late. Ironically, in my hometown, that was normal. I rebelled in a different way. I decided that I would put my head down and work hard so I could get out of society's expectations and standards as fast as possible. I put in the work while my classmates went to weekend parties and watched volleyball games. This was the first step I took to get out of my comfort zone and on my way to an extraordinary life. This was the first step in my journey to becoming my most badass self.

Now that I have pushed past my comfort zone and have immersed myself in the tools I need to continue to push past that barrier, I can see simply that I am on my journey toward an extraordinary life and everything I have dreamed of. As I teach you how to embark on your own journey, I want to make it crystal clear that this is for anyone who is seeking a change or something different from the status quo you were born into. Furthermore, I am no different. You and I are very much the same. We are two people who are seeking something bigger and chasing the voice inside us. Once I started making changes to my own life, I couldn't stand the idea of not sharing what I have learned with others. In fact, I believe that I was put on this earth to teach others. That is my "Big Why" (more on that later). I hope that I can provide some clarity on what it takes to get to that extraordinary life and that by learning from my journey and applying the tools to your own challenges and experiences, you will be well on your way to achieving an extraordinary life of your own.

I took my experiences, hardships, and tragedies and wrapped them up nice and neat into this book—a manual of sorts—so that you can skip that uncertainty and reach that badass life that I know you desire so deeply. *You* deserve to live that extraordinary life. I want to give you a head start on what you're about to endure so it won't take you as long to achieve it as it took me. I had to fumble around in the dark to learn enough to open the door to my extraordinary life and, through this book, I am holding the flashlight to illuminate what it will take for you to do the same.

MY EXTRAORDINARY LIFE DID NOT COME LOOKING FOR ME, JUST LIKE IT WON'T COME LOOKING FOR YOU.

I had to go get it, just as you will. To achieve that, I had to push to the other side of my comfort zone. I had to crawl out from the bottom of my crab bucket and fight everything that was holding me back.

I can think back to the moment when everything pivoted for me and I discovered what I needed to start my journey. See, it wasn't until I discovered the crab bucket theory, and started researching exactly how to get out of it, that I understood what was happening to me and those I grew up with. We are going to talk about the crab bucket theory in more detail soon; for now, understand that this theory is what explains everything you have likely been feeling. It describes exactly how and why you've been held back from your fullest potential. When I dug deep into the psychology behind it, I finally understood why everyone was stuck in the same place, with no hope or desire to go after a bigger and better life for themselves. This moment was a giant smack to the face, as if the universe was trying to hit me hard enough so I would finally wake up and start listening. I had to break myself loose from experiences, people, and environments in order to reach my extraordinary life, and you will too.

To get out of my bucket, I had to break myself loose from being poor, undereducated, and unfulfilled, wondering what was wrong with me and why I just couldn't fit in. Wondering if I would ever truly be happy or if I would ever achieve that lifestyle I'd dreamed so fiercely for since I was a little kid.

By doing the things I am going to teach you throughout this book, I went from broke, unhappy, traumatized, and unfulfilled to a top-producing real estate agent, multiple business owner, and published author all before the age of twenty. I have left in the past what no longer serves me, and I have a clear roadmap of how to reach the extraordinary life I have always dreamed of. I have come so far, and I am immensely proud of the progress I have made, yet there's so much farther I still want to go. Now, I am happy, fulfilled, and excited to take the world by storm. I am living a life that

I don't need a vacation from, and the Madison I was 3–4 years ago would have stared up at who I am now and said, "That's who I want to be!"

As we embark on this journey together, I want to be 100 percent transparent with you. As I wrote this book, I found it difficult to talk about some of the things I have experienced because I am still in it, every single day. I constantly fight against the tiny voices in the back of my head yelling at me, saying, "Who the hell are you to be writing about this?" "How am I supposed to teach others how to reach their extraordinary life when I am still working toward mine?" But that's the whole point, isn't it? As you are working on this journey, take comfort in knowing that I am right alongside you. We are on this journey together.

As you work through this transformation, I believe that you will experience a powerful shift, just like I did. By starting the project of becoming your most badass self, to reach your extraordinary life, and by doing the necessary work to leave what no longer serves you, almost every aspect of your life is going to become very clear. When I did finally break out of what was holding me back with an undeniable vision of what my future held for me, I moved away from those comforts very quickly, as though they were always meant to go. Don't be surprised when people and environments start to shift rapidly.

The stories that I am going to share with you weren't that long ago for me, yet it feels like decades. That is how powerful this transformation is. Experiences I thought had changed me forever are now foggy memories that no longer serve me. I expect that you will go through this similar and powerful shift.

So that's my promise, folks. I will show you the pathway to first discovering the things that hold you back, and then letting go of what no longer serves you. Once you are able to break through your comfort zone, I will show you the stepping-stones to your extraordinary life.

For the first part of our time together, we'll discuss our mindset before we actually take the actionable steps that we discuss later in this book. If you were to skip the first part of this book and not complete the exercises, you would find the second part of this book is not as effective as it could be. The discussion on mindset is about first recognizing what you cannot carry with you in this journey and what would otherwise be really happy to hold you back from reaching your extraordinary life.

WHAT IS HOLDING YOU BACK FROM YOUR EXTRAORDINARY LIFE?

In order to start the journey toward your extraordinary life, it's imperative to understand what exactly is holding you back. The crab bucket theory is the key that will unlock your understanding of everything that keeps you from growing forward. The crab bucket theory is this: when a single crab is put into a bucket without a lid, they can easily escape and, undoubtedly, they will. It's in their nature. However, once that crab is accompanied by one, two, three, or more crabs, not a single one of the crabs will be able to escape the lidless bucket. It doesn't matter how many crabs are in the bucket, if there are more than one, they cannot escape. This bucket could be full to the brim of crabs, and yet their nature will no longer let them escape this bucket. What was once such a simple, mindless task for the lone crab is now impossible for the multitudes.

By nature, these crabs are still going to try to reach the top of the bucket to escape. But once one crab begins to crawl its way out and pull itself above the other crabs, the others will claw and scratch at that crab, dragging him back to the bottom of the bucket. The theory is simple. We, as human beings, are the crabs trying to escape. Our careers, our upbringing, our friends, our family, and our environment are the crabs clawing and pulling us back down. I want you to picture this vividly, as this journey will be a battle, a fight to release the roadblocks and finally have the opportunity to move forward.

So, what's the psychology behind this? Crabs did not evolve in buckets but rather on the seashore, clinging to each other. This act promoted their survival because there is safety in numbers. When in the bucket, they are repeating the same behavior they were naturally selected for: clinging to each other to survive. In this new environment, the behavior that would normally protect them now holds them back.

Other animal species also cling to one another for their own safety, such as mammals. Mammals (including humans) often seek safety in numbers to stay protected from predators. Natural selection has built a brain that rewards social support and makes you feel physically uncomfortable when your support is threatened. Our brains make us feel good when we stay in a group of people or environment we deem as "safe." Breaking out of the mold feels wrong and dangerous.

Just like a cub that clings to its mother for safety and security, humans do the same. This science is why someone with the intelligence to become an Ivy League graduate, but who grew up in a poorer, crime-filled neighborhood, will instead likely continue to be stuck in their "bucket"—their environment that makes them feel safe and comfortable. That's where they have been born and raised, just like their parents, grandparents, and generations before them. They stay in this poor neighborhood because it's comfortable and familiar. Their brain makes them feel good because it believes there is safety with their friends and family. It doesn't matter to us that we are sacrificing our potential to stay in what's comfortable. Even though someone who decides to spend their weekend drinking and partying instead of learning and growing most likely understands that their habits are destructive to their success, it doesn't matter because their brain gives off a chemical that makes them feel good when they stay in their bucket. Those that are stuck in the bucket aren't self-aware enough to realize that they are sacrificing their potential by staying where they feel safe. If they were aware, they would make a change.

Before this transformational journey,

I WAS JUST ANOTHER CRAB STUCK IN THE BOTTOM OF THE BUCKET, NOT QUITE UNDERSTANDING WHY I WAS THERE AND WHAT WAS KEEPING ME DOWN.

I remember observing in my hometown the same repetitive pattern that was expected from me, the pattern that was considered normal. This environment I had grown up in was a prime example of the crabs in a bucket, and I was just one crab clinging to what was comfortable.

What are you clinging to? What exactly is holding you back from all that you desire? You're reading this book because you feel like you haven't reached your full potential and that the extraordinary life you have been dreaming of is waiting for you. In reading this book, I hope to share the lessons I've learned so far (the successes and failures), and I hope these lessons help you break free from what's holding you back, achieve a greater mindset, and create a roadmap of what your extraordinary life really is. In fact, if you take the things you learn in this book, it *will* change your mindset and in turn, your life. However, the only way the change will come is if you take the lessons and tools taught in this book and *take action*. The world is unpredictable; the only thing we have control over is ourselves. It's time to take the leap. I'll say this more than once throughout the course of the book, but listen to this truth, and listen hard: everything you want in life, *everything*, is on the other side of your comfort zone. The only way to grow is to get uncomfortable, and the only way to get uncomfortable is to take action.

This book is going to make you uncomfortable, so before you turn to the rest of what I have to say, I want you to get sold. Get sold on this journey and get sold on committing to spending time on yourself and what it really takes to achieve your extraordinary life. After all, if you picked up this book, there is a part of you, no matter how big or small, that is looking for something greater than what you have now.

What does it mean to be "sold"? It's to commit to putting forth the effort of learning the necessary steps and to have an open mind when it comes to the theory of the crabs and how it affects you and your everyday life, as well as how to utilize these tools to reach your extraordinary life you have dreamed about. The second part is taking what I teach you and putting it into action so that these actions may be the first stepping-stone toward what changes your life forever.

It's time to commit to taking whatever action is necessary. Read what I have to say, take the lessons in this book, and put them into action. I want you to use this book as a manual or guideline. Get your highlighter or pen out, because you will be using it throughout this book, and make sure to mark the sections you might need to come back to. Once you've read it once, use it as a reference guide to taking that action that will change your life. This book is going to become personal to you, a journal of sorts, so make the best use of the lessons I have put together for you and take the necessary action. I hope at this point you've heard just enough to spend the next several hours with me and this book and to commit to unlocking Project Badass. Are you ready?

PART 1
DISCOVERING YOUR BUCKET

1

RECOGNIZE THE SIGNS

GROWING UP IN MY FAMILY, THE EXPECTATION FOR ME AND MY sister was to be married and pregnant right out of high school—to make my mother a grandmother before the age of forty, as she did to her mother, and her mother did to my great-grandmother. This was never discussed; it was just something we all subconsciously knew was normal in our family. This path, for my sister and I, was predictable and safe.

So it wasn't a surprise to my family when I announced, at age seventeen, that I was engaged to my high school sweetheart and anxiously awaiting my eighteenth birthday when we could marry. This was normal. This was the bucket that I was born into. No one would be surprised if we had announced that we were expecting in the months following the wedding. It was expected of me to follow the same pattern as generations before. It was so easy for me to make the decision of getting married and starting a family, because my brain knew this was safe and predictable, so it released oxytocin, making me feel good. At the bottom of my bucket, tucked safely into my comfort zone, it was easy to look inward and take the expected actions instead of pushing against the norm for the extraordinary life I have always thought about.

When we stay in the bucket, we feel good, we feel safe, and we feel comfortable. But remember what I said about being comfortable? Everything is on the other side of your comfort zone. In fact . . .

THE COMFORT ZONE = THE CRAB BUCKET

Everything you want is just over the lip of that bucket, and you are now standing at the bottom, looking at light peeking through the top.

After years, decades, and even a lifetime of this repetitive action, we begin to believe that there is no other way out, that being stuck at the bottom of the bucket is just the way it is. Even more unfortunate, most are oblivious that we are even stuck in a bucket—or stuck in the comfortable repetitive actions we take. Feel-good behavior is *exactly* what is holding you back from reaching your badass self.

The strategies to unlock your full potential are written out in this book for you. Knowing this truth, and not acting upon it? I don't think I could live with that knowledge and continue to stay comfortable at the bottom of my bucket. If you have committed to unlocking your full potential, and are honestly ready to do whatever it takes, know that it is going to take determination and grit. It's not going to be easy. It is the hardest thing I have ever done. It is not a straight path from the bottom of your bucket to the top. Unlocking your full potential and extraordinary life is messy, hard, and sometimes painful.

Because we've acted the same way for years upon years, and throughout generations, our subconscious mind believes that we will always be stuck in the bucket. It's time to rewire that. If your subconscious mind believes something, then that is the way it will be. My subconscious mind believed that getting married and starting a family at such a young age was my path, because that's what was comfortable. The subconscious mind is a powerful tool, whether it's working for or against you. It all depends on how you use it. We will dive, in-depth, into learning how the subconscious mind contributes to keeping us in the bucket. And, more importantly, how you can use it to get out.

Getting out of the bucket is going to be an immense challenge, and the first step is going to be recognizing the signs that you are, undoubtedly, stuck in the bucket. Once you are able to recognize the signs, you will be able to move forward in order to eliminate all of the factors that are keeping you there:

- Victim Mentality
- No Direction or Reason (a.k.a., "no purpose" in life)
- Financial Limitations
- Dwelling on Past Trauma
- Not "Fitting In"

Just to preface this, I exuded each one of these traits before getting out of the bucket. I practiced these common signs of someone stuck in my comfort zone daily.

VICTIM MENTALITY

A victim mentality is feeling as though every negative thing that happens to you is someone else's fault. In short, it's not owning your own shit. For example, you may go throughout your days feeling as though your friend is out to get you. Or perhaps something goes wrong at work because your coworker didn't do this or that. Maybe it's blaming your bad credit score on your boss not paying you enough money. Whatever it is, having a victim mentality is an energy-sucking hole where potential goes to shrivel up and die. You might not recognize it right away, but if you've ever heard yourself say, "Well, it's not my fault," then you probably have a victim mentality—and it's time to own your shit.

A great quote to explain this, from the book *Extreme Ownership*, says, "Once people stop making excuses, stop blaming others, and take ownership of everything in their lives, they are compelled to take action to solve their problems."

NO DIRECTION OR REASON

When you're coasting along in life with no real passion, drive, or goals and no feeling of "purpose," you're probably stuck in the bucket. It might look a little like this: you have a job that pays the bills and a decent roof over your head. Your wife cooks you dinner, and afterward you sit on the couch and watch a movie or TV with the kids, dreading the moment when the clock strikes 9:30 p.m. because you will soon be laying your head on the pillow—and, moments later, waking up and walking into work again. Weekends are filled with Monday Dread, as the clock strikes 4:00 p.m. on Sunday evening and you beg the minutes to tick by slower so you don't have to start your week over again.

This, folks, is coasting. You're not sure exactly why you get up every day and go to a job you despise (other than to make ends meet). In fact, the only sensible reason is that you do these things because that's what you are "supposed to do." You might have always wondered why this is the way things are but have never had the drive to get up and find out why. You have no reason to find your calling because at the bottom of the bucket, where you have been coasting for numerous years, it's comfortable and safe. This seemingly meaningless routine is easy to follow because there is no risk. You are stuck in the bucket, and as we've talked about before, your brain makes you feel good when staying in your comfort zone.

FINANCIAL LIMITATIONS

This is a big one, one that I am very, very passionate about. I grew up in a poor family; we lived paycheck to paycheck, barely making ends meet, and the topic of our finances (rather, the topic of not having enough money) was a common discussion around the dinner table or anytime something we needed cost any money. To my mother and step-father's credit, we always had food on our table and clothes on our backs, but I know that there were many nights they lay awake at night worried if they could keep the heat on or make the rent payment that month. I was raised to believe that the wealthy were evil and that I would never experience what it was like to be financially healthy, because that's just how it is. We didn't want "rich people problems" anyway, right? We wouldn't want to worry about paying taxes or handling the extra stress of multiple income streams. That just wasn't something we wanted. It was easier to stay where we were and not risk our "security." I never learned how to use money or how to manage it as the wealthy do, and the only way I learned how to make money was to go to work and earn an hourly wage.

I was stuck in the bucket of my inherited mindset about money: get a job working for someone else and be satisfied with $10 an hour. If I had a newish car with a manageable car payment and a decent roof over my head, that was leaps and bounds ahead of expectations.

One of my good friends mentioned to me that he felt like his money mindset was the one thing holding him back from reaching his success. Like myself, he was raised to believe that "money is evil" and that "rich people are greedy and immoral" and that, more than anything, he needed to "stay in his lane." He also surrounded himself with people that, although (possibly) well-meaning, were extremely unsupportive and judgmental. This included family, friends, and his spouse. It is very hard to change your mindsets about money and to pursue your dreams when your loved ones are telling you money is evil, telling you to not work so hard, acting jealous over your success, and attempting to sabotage your success under the guise of being caring or concerned.

Just as my friend confirmed, once you get serious about escaping the bucket to realize your full potential, you will start to "earn haters," as Grant Cardone likes to say. Friends, family, coworkers: they all can turn into grasping crabs desperate to pull you back down. It will seem like they drift down a different path because you, in fact, took a different turn than those around you. When I started seeking the knowledge, mindset, and mentorship of the successful, I started to earn haters. These people hated the fact that I was looking for a way to build my empire and that I was breaking out of the generational mold of hourly wages to work for myself and prioritize creating wealth for myself.

DWELLING ON PAST TRAUMA

Another clear sign of being stuck in the bucket is dwelling on your past trauma and not being able to move on. You may *want* to move on from what happened to you, but you're not quite sure how or aren't willing to risk the hurt that it might cause. You might also be dwelling on the trauma you endured so much that you blame it on everyone else (see the section about "victim mentality" above). My past trauma is something, to this day, that I must continue to work through. One of the most painful experiences I had was also one of the most life-changing. I was sexually assaulted by a friend from my high school—someone I thought I could trust. I can't speak to what his intentions were or why he did it. But something inside me broke.

Once you experience something like sexual assault, it changes your mindset completely. You can no longer pretend like the once-friendly hands that touched you, his hands, were touching out of care rather than malice. You also have the knowledge ingrained in you that his hands touched your skin. This experience made me feel used, like a crumpled-up tissue thrown to the side.

Unfortunately, it was not just a one-time act. It was continuous manipulation, emotional abuse, and nonconsensual sexual acts. I was so desperate to be loved and to finally be accepted that I let it continue. He forced me to pleasure him sexually before giving me a hug or kiss or any sort of affection. He refused to acknowledge my existence if I didn't want to have sex with him. I was so stressed that I couldn't eat without getting sick. I should have stopped it after the first time, but because I was so stuck in my crab bucket, I accepted the "love" I thought I deserved.

The time with him wasn't all bad, although the good wasn't enough to outweigh the bad. I know that now, but I didn't know it then. He would buy me gifts, take me out on nice dates, and always replace the dying flowers with live ones to make sure I knew—and everyone else around me knew—how good I had it.

But he showed his true colors to me, of course. I was blind to it to begin with, but my vision got clearer and clearer as I grasped onto little things that helped me crawl out of this bucket. He was envious of my successes and wouldn't support me in anything I was trying to accomplish because it made him look less than.

When I finally saw that shard of peeking light, I was able to finally, finally break off the relationship. *He* was the one who cried, the one who was heartbroken. Suddenly, I was the liar, the cheater, the manipulator. We never spoke about the abuse.

I didn't tell a soul about what happened for well over a year after I had ended it. Why? I think it was because I was in mourning. Something nobody talks about, when getting out of the crab bucket, is that your entire existence still yearns for the bucket, the toxic thing, even with the full realization that it no longer serves you. Have you ever wondered why abuse victims keep going back? Because the abuser is familiar, and once you get out, you're heartbroken and vulnerable and everything feels uncomfortable. Additionally, despite the fact that abuse victims know that it is destructive, our brains trick us into thinking the destructive cycle is okay, simply because it is familiar.

So, *how* did I get out of this bucket? As a victim of abuse, it was incredibly hard for me to leave this relationship, despite being miserable and hurting. However, I knew the person I wanted to be and the life I wanted to live. I was a high school student, just a short handful of months away from being able to work toward the life I so deeply desired to live. I could see, clearly, the woman I wanted to be. Who she was, what she did, how she lived. At the end, I knew in my heart that being with this person, and succumbing to the familiar abuse, was not going to allow me to get to that life. Even knowing this didn't make the leaving any easier. The expectation was for us to stay together through college, and I would have lowered my level of success to what he deemed acceptable. We would have gotten married and pregnant. Then, thirty years down the road, I would be in an unhealthy, abusive marriage. Stuck in the familiarity, with children who didn't deserve to grow up in that environment, stupidly loving a man who didn't love me back. In that scenario, I would have been miles and miles away from the woman I *needed* to be to fulfill my purpose. So I convinced my subconscious mind of the woman I wanted to be and got out of the bucket by committing to making that a reality and doing whatever it took until I got there. By getting out of this bucket and moving past this traumatic experience, it opened up the door to meet my future husband, which is an entirely different lesson I was set to learn. We will discuss that later on.

NOT "FITTING IN"

Having the feeling that you don't fit in is a clear sign of being stuck in the bucket. Your subconscious mind is telling you that you belong somewhere else, somewhere outside of the bucket. The most distinct memories I have from my childhood are the ones where I felt like I was standing on the outside looking in, the memories where I wished I was prettier, shorter, had more friends or richer parents. Unfortunately, I wasn't taught the value of finding the uniqueness in yourself and loving it, and I definitely wasn't taught to be comfortable in the uncomfortable. I remember standing in the middle school hallway, teased because I chose to read instead of gossip. I was mocked in high school because I chose to study rather than go to the weekend party. Honestly, I was never invited to those parties anyway because people thought I was "stuck up," a high school student with a chip on my shoulder. The few friends I did make through school and childhood are no longer a part of my life because, as I pulled myself out of my bucket, they were the first to become haters. I won't play the victim; it sucked—but I was strong enough to listen to my subconscious mind saying, "Keep grinding, you'll get out of this place soon enough and life will be so much better." I knew I belonged elsewhere, outside of that comfort zone.

As we work through the remaining exercises in this book, recognizing these common traits of being stuck in the bucket will make it much easier to discover what your specific buckets are and what it's going to take to get you out and move forward. Lawrence Bossidy said, "Self-awareness enables you to learn from your mistakes as well as your successes. It enables you to keep growing." I think you'll now find it much easier to recognize when you are exhibiting traits of being stuck in the bucket, or when others are. It's much like seeing a red truck after you've purchased one for yourself: You can't seem to remember ever seeing them driving on the freeway before, but now that you're driving one yourself, you notice a red truck every time you drive to work or run errands. By understanding and being aware of these common traits of being stuck in the bucket, you'll start to find that you are seeing them on a regular basis—in yourself and others.

2

OTHERS' EXPECTATIONS

THROUGHOUT THIS JOURNEY OF SHIFTING YOUR MINDSET AND getting out of your comfort zone, you will notice a couple of things. As we've already discussed, you're going to earn haters and naysayers. You're going to start hearing a lot of things from people who are still in the bucket, and what they have to say is going to be negative. You are going to wonder why you are putting yourself out there, when it is so much easier and more comfortable to just stay in the bucket and keep floating on by. You will have the thought of "Why don't I just be like everyone else?" I know this because the same thing ran through my head. "*Should* I just settle?" That shit can eat away at your soul. When you aren't totally and fully comfortable in being you, it hurts and it's tempting to run away in the other direction, to something seemingly safer. But remember, you are uncomfortable because you are growing and changing, and that is a good thing.

Something that bugged the hell out of me through my journey was puzzling over why the majority of society follow the status quo and, ultimately, stay inside the crab bucket while chastising the few who try to crawl out. That question poked and prodded at me for weeks until I finally sat down to find out why. I sought out an explanation from everywhere I could: books, mentors, podcasts. Here's the truth—the ones still in the bucket are the people who are too afraid or too weak to realize they are simply coasting through life.

THESE PEOPLE PULL YOU DOWN BECAUSE THEY CAN'T STAND THAT YOU ARE GRIPPING ONTO THE EDGE OF THAT BUCKET AND PULLING YOURSELF TO YOUR FULL POTENTIAL WITH EVERY OUNCE OF STRENGTH INSIDE YOUR BODY.

I had to teach myself not to take this personally. These types of people aren't upset with you; in fact, they aren't even focused on you. They are focused on themselves, ashamed of knowing that they are letting fear hold them back from their full potential. They may even have the smallest, quietest voice in the back of their head asking why they don't try to get out of the bucket, but they continue to ignore it.

As far back as I can remember, there was always a voice inside me yelling at me to get out of my bucket, even before I understood what that meant. The voice inside me kept telling me to push faster, harder, and farther. Despite the fact that society praises the comfortability of living life on autopilot, I always felt the need to make waves. Why would I wait, why would I coast and stay complacent? The ones waiting for the right time are the people still stuck in the crab bucket. If you keep waiting for the right time, you'll wait forever. Make waves and do it now.

My mother often says, "Just slow down, Madison." To my mother, I love you, but dammit, I am not going to slow down! I want my extraordinary life to happen now. I wanted it to happen yesterday. Now that I am out of the bucket, I have such a clear vision of my life, my goals, my passion, the thing that sets my soul on fire—why would I wait to reach my extraordinary life? Our time here is short and neither you nor I have time to wait until it's "right." In fact, I need to know that if I died tomorrow, I did everything in my power to reach my highest potential. When you are in your comfort zone you are stagnant. Sure, the comfort zone feels like a safe place to wait until the "right time" comes around. Unfortunately, that big, red-faced bastard known as the "right time" never comes knocking at your door with opportunity. Even though the comfort zone is where success goes to die, we are wired to relish in the safety net of waiting. Waiting until you get out of college before pursuing any sort of career? Bullshit. Starting a new venture in your forties, don't you dare—you've already missed your time. Complete and utter bullshit!

The time is now! If you've ever wanted to start a business but you think you're too young, just do it now. If you've ever wanted to switch careers but think that you're too old, just do it now. If you've ever wanted to leave your spouse but are afraid of abandoning the last ten years of comfort behind—do it now! Growth dies in your comfort zone. As Bob Proctor said, "If you're not moving forward, you're moving backward." Get uncomfortable with the fact that waiting for the "right time" is a lie. Don't let anyone—not your parents, brothers, friends, sisters, or anyone—dictate the timeline of your life. Take it into your own hands. No one else will do it for you.

I want you to think about the wildly successful people of this world, the ones that leave their legacy behind. Think of your top three idols or role models that fit into that category. Now, I want you to answer these questions honestly. Are these people average? Are these people following society's status quo? If your answer to any of these three questions is "yes," you're lying to yourself. No, these people are not average. They are the radical, the obsessed, the crazy, the lunatic people who decided to wave a big middle finger to the rest of the world and tell everyone to "Fuck off, I'm doing what I am passionate about."

Guaranteed, those people also thought, "Why am I not like everyone else?" They just decided that their passion was stronger than their doubts and fears. They decided to get uncomfortable, and they learned to embrace it. Now they are wealthy from it in more ways than one. I can't speak for you, but that sounds great to me. These people cracked the code! They know the secret sauce to following their passion and achieving massive levels of extraordinary success.

I am going to help you learn what makes you extraordinary. Just like the wildly successful people before you, you will have naysayers and haters. They will always have something negative to say as you continue on this journey toward your extraordinary life. But once you can fully grasp what makes you extraordinary, you must use it to your advantage in every way you can, and not give a damn about the expectations of others. This might look like using what you're passionate about to start a business, start investing in real estate, or maybe start a charity for something close to your heart. Don't let one more minute pass by without doing everything in your power to reach your utmost potential and succeed in greater ways than you, or anyone else around you, thought was possible. In today's society, we are so fortunate to have the opportunity to create something out of nothing. To start a business, a movement, or a brand revolving around the one thing that makes you great, that thing that makes your heart sing. Refuse to let anyone else's expectations sway your pathway to greatness. Make the decision to get out of your bucket and strive for your potential. I made the decision to put my middle fingers up to the world, and to other people's expectations. Why do I feel that way?

IT'S SIMPLE—
I REFUSE TO LIVE A LIFE THAT'S
ANYTHING BUT EXTRAORDINARY.

3

BREAK THE CYCLE

YOU MAY NOT HAVE BEEN BORN INTO A WEALTHY FAMILY, OR maybe you weren't raised with the mindset of success and abundance. Most of us weren't. I certainly wasn't. Regardless that you weren't born into it or taught it from a young age, you are the one that is reading this book and taking the first steps toward breaking that cycle that has loomed for generations. The first hurdle to getting out of the bucket is realizing that you are, in fact, stuck at the bottom. In order to break free, you need to figure out exactly what your comfort zone is and what is keeping you there. This is going to be a self-discovery process—a personal journey.

It may be different for everyone, but for me the biggest hurdle that kept me in my bucket was the people around me. There are always those select few people in your life that have the biggest impact on you, positive or negative. As children, we are malleable. We follow by example and learn from behaviors. Before getting out of the bucket, I didn't quite understand how important it was to be selective with the people you let influence you. In fact, humans are like dough, where each hand that touches our life molds us into the hard crust of an adult.

Because people had a huge impact on what has held me back in the past, I still have to be conscious of the people I let in my life to this day. It is my nature to be greatly affected by those around me. My story has a lot of highlighted characters . . . parents, boyfriends, mentors, husbands, and friends that all had a hand in creating the person I am today. In my experience, those traumatic experiences loomed bigger and darker than those who positively impacted me. But the biggest tragedies create the most beautiful masterpieces. Some of the most breathtaking works of art were born from the darkest places.

I think the darkest moments of our lives create the strongest armor on our backs. These moments, regardless of the trauma you faced to conquer them, shaped you into the person you are today and provided you with a shield that will push you forward even on the hardest days. Once you get out of the bucket, and after layers and layers of armor, you are self-aware enough to start to form a list of crab buckets you refuse to succumb to again. In my situation, these experiences taught me that the only person I need is myself. My independent happiness is the most important thing. At the end of the day, I am the only one who has to live with myself. Maybe that's selfish, maybe that's arrogant, but I know enough now to not care. I also know that I must break the cycle and be very careful of what is threatening to push me back into my comfort zone.

I wish that it was a simple black-and-white decision to determine the boundaries you must put in place to keep yourself from tipping backward into your bucket. However, it is not that easy; life is messy. It's red, gray, yellow, and every other color under the rainbow.

Because life is not black and white, it is critical to know the triggers that could send you crashing back over the edge. It is critical to determine what your buckets are. Who is it? What is it? Is it a location, a person, an activity, a mindset? We've talked about the people in our lives that can hold us in the bottom of the bucket, but just as easily—your surroundings, activities, habits, and mindset can keep you struggling at the bottom. We'll talk more about that later.

Once you determine what triggers you to shift back into your comfort zone, run as far as possible away from that trigger.

GET INTO THE MINDSET THAT YOU'D RATHER DIE THAN FALL BACK INTO THE BUCKET AND SCRAPE ROCK BOTTOM AGAIN.

This mindset is what will propel you forward. That every damn day, you will wake up and do everything in your power to stay away from the bucket. Every decision you make should move the needle forward, not backward.

I want you to imagine it like this. Your crab bucket is stacked underneath another bucket, and then another, and another. All the way up. Once you get out of one bucket, somehow and someway, you find yourself at the bottom of your next bucket. Will we ever truly get out of the bucket, completely? To some stage of "enlightenment," so to speak?

I couldn't say. Does that mean we stop trying to claw our way out? No. We keep going. Continuously ask yourself, "What bucket am I in, and how do I get out?" The more buckets you get out of, the better a person you will grow to be. I'm not sure if you can ever reach the top of the tower, to look down at the dozens of buckets stacked beneath you. I honestly couldn't tell you, because I haven't reached the top yet. In my opinion, you will never reach the top. That is the beautiful thing about being human, you have the opportunity to *never* be stagnant, to always move forward, grow, and improve yourself. Unfortunately, it's only the few that understand that you must continue to climb up and up and up. Most people just coast along the bottom of the bucket, wherever that may be.

The two key lessons from this chapter to help you break the cycle:

1. The people around you have a direct impact on your life and the bucket you are stuck in. These people could be impacting you negatively or positively. Choose wisely.

2. Our subconscious mind and our overall mindset (as discussed more in detail later on) are *the* single most powerful tool you have to get out of the bucket.

Keeping these in mind will be imperative as you start to discover your bucket and break the cycle that has been holding you, and possibly generations before you, back from reaching your full potential and extraordinary life. I've shared a few of the things that have kept me in the bucket before. And as I stated at the beginning of this chapter, you first must discover your bucket and who/what is keeping you there in order to break the cycle. As uncomfortable as it may be, I want you to write it down. I have reserved a few blank pages for you to start discovering your bucket and to discover your triggers. Just start brain dumping. This book is meant to be consumed in parts and for you to take action as you go. Before you move on, stop and discover your bucket. Do it now.

Here are a few questions to answer as you are completing this exercise. As you answer these for yourself, I think you'll find that it will prompt you to expand further and open your eyes to other things that could be holding you back.

- "Who in my life is holding me back from my dreams?"
- "Is there a specific location or surrounding that succumbs me to making decisions that don't support my bigger vision?"
- "What experiences (good or bad) haven't been dealt with or are something that holds me back from making daily progress?"

DISCOVERING YOUR BUCKET

If you're reading this part, I expect you have the first exercise done: discovering your bucket. Knowing exactly what is holding you back from your full potential makes it impossible to ignore. That exercise most likely made you uncomfortable, and that's a good thing. Why? Because *everything* you want is on the *other side* of your comfort zone.

Keep these triggers at the front of your mind as we move through the next exercises. Now that you are increasingly self-aware of your crab buckets, you can use the following tools to finally move forward and thrive in your extraordinary life.

PART 2

THE TOOLS TO THRIVE

THIS NEXT PART OF THE BOOK IS GOING TO BE A LITTLE LIKE being on a diet. There are going to be days where you want to cheat and fall back into the comfortable, destructive habits that have kept you in the bucket for this long. When these temptations come, don't let them overtake you. Find this book and read through the steps again. There are still days where I feel myself teetering on the edge of the bucket, but don't let the security of being comfortable overtake you. Just remember, *everything* you want is on the other side of your comfort zone.

4

SOMETHING BIGGER
THAN YOURSELF

NOW THAT YOU ARE ABLE TO CLEARLY RECOGNIZE YOUR TRIG-
gers and what is keeping you stuck, it's time to eliminate
them. In order to crawl out of your bucket, you first need to
be clear on what you are doing this for and why these bad
habits are keeping you from achieving your most badass self
and that extraordinary life. Once this is clear, you are able to
determine that everything you do moving forward is to serve
your "Big Why."

A "Big Why" is the driving force behind getting up every
single day and pushing through obstacles. It's the reason you
keep going even when you hit a ceiling, rubbing your fin-
gerprints on the glass, peering ahead and wondering exactly
how to break through the boundary in front of you.. This is
your statement of purpose, your calling, your mission statement. This purpose drives your decisions, lifestyle, career
choice, etc.

I truly believe, with all of my heart, that we were all
put on this Earth to teach each other something. We are all

here for something bigger than ourselves, something bigger than the money, the big house, the fancy car. At the end of your life, wouldn't you want to feel utterly fulfilled—that you did everything in your damn power to reach your highest potential?

A good friend of mine once asked me, "Besides the money, why do you do this?" It was a great question, a fair question. Your "Big Why" is important. It is what propels you forward on the bad days and motivates you to get even better on the good ones.

There is something bigger than myself, a calling that I am supposed to fulfill.

I BELIEVE THAT I WAS PUT ON THIS EARTH TO TEACH OTHERS HOW TO GET OUT OF THEIR COMFORT ZONE AND BREAK THROUGH EVERY BOUNDARY IN FRONT OF THEM— SELF-MADE OR SOCIETY-MADE.

I am meant to teach others that whatever excuse they have, it is not a reason to give up. I don't give a damn if you think you're too young or too old, not rich enough, or not smart enough. It *is* possible to follow the clues that success leaves and create your own destiny, to fulfill your calling.

What is your "Big Why"? Have you determined that yet? If you haven't, now is the time. What legacy do you have to leave? What sets your soul on fire, to the point that every time you think about it and envision what that could look like, you can barely contain the excitement, joy, and pride you feel? After fully discovering my "Big Why," I realized that every single day, all I had to do was push the needle forward, closer toward my "Big Why." The realization was so simple, and so profound, it changed my life forever.

Success is simple, not easy. It's simple to get up and make moves that bring you closer to that calling, but it is not easy to get up and repeat the same consistent actions over and over again, especially when every fiber of your being is telling you to go back to what's comfortable and safe. With your "Big Why," consistently showing up is 80 percent of the battle. If you can get behind the idea that consistency and taking action is what will create that lasting success, you've already won.

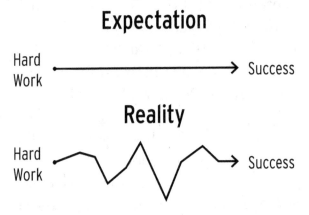

It's time to commit to your "Big Why" and to yourself. It would be a tragedy to let your dreams slide by. So commit to yourself, commit to consistently showing up every day to move the needle forward in fulfilling your "Big Why." Don't let your crab bucket be the reason you don't commit to yourself and your calling. That's what the average person is doing! They are scared, worried, nervous, and doubting themselves. I imagine you are feeling all of those things too, but taking action despite these feelings is what will set you apart. If you continue to remain in your bucket, you'll be stuck with those others who aren't doing a damn thing either.

Let's determine your "Big Why." Right here, right now. No excuses, no "I don't have enough time" or "I'll do it later." Are you committed? Are you sold on yourself? Yes! Then do it now, before moving on to the next chapter. It might be hard to imagine how we are going to narrow down to exactly what your "Big Why" is. Also, it might feel a bit overwhelming. Don't worry! We are going to start by thinking broadly, and then we will narrow it down further. To make it easier, I will tell you what my "Big Why" is, so that you can further understand the goal of these exercises.

For me, teaching and coaching entrepreneurs was one of the five passions I listed here, and my "Big Why." I knew the value I could bring to others and the legacy I could leave. I knew by providing this value, it would create lasting wealth for my family and generations beyond me. It would provide the extraordinary life I have always wanted. By doing this, I would not only be serving other entrepreneurs, but I would also create freedom for myself.

Start by listing the top five things you are passionate about. This can be anything. Write them here, now.

5 THINGS I AM PASSIONATE ABOUT

1. _____

_____

_____

_____

2. _____

_____

_____

_____

3. _____

_____

_____

_____

4. _____

_____

_____

_____

5. _____

_____

_____

_____

Great, now review your list. As we discussed, we are taking this from a large overview before breaking it down into a micro view. In this next exercise, I want you to write a brief description of how you could use each passion and what that would do for you. What value can you bring to others? What can you teach them? What makes you stand out from the crowd that gives you the courage and confidence to share this skill? Now, you may already be dabbling in these things, especially if you are passionate about them, but it's time to think about what legacy you could leave behind by using this passion to your fullest potential.

For each of these five skills, I want you to close your eyes and cast the vision of what living your passion to the utmost potential would look like. Who are you, what are you doing, where are you? Then I want you to think about what that does for you. What does your lifestyle look like? Who are you doing it for (family, children, generations, etc.)? Lastly, what would it feel like if you accomplished this?

CAST MY VISION

1. _____
   _____
   _____
   _____
   _____
   _____
   _____
   _____
   _____
   _____
   _____
   _____

2. _____
   _____
   _____
   _____
   _____
   _____
   _____
   _____
   _____
   _____
   _____
   _____
   _____
   _____
   _____

3. _____

4. _____

5. _____

_____

_____

_____

_____

_____

_____

_____

_____

_____

_____

_____

_____

Focusing on yourself and thinking about what you truly want can be challenging when society teaches that doing so is selfish. With an open mind, I want you to look back at those five items, all with different outcomes, lifestyles, and levels of fulfilment. Get really honest with yourself. Which of these passions sets your soul on fire? When I cast the vision of my why, my goals, and my lifestyle, I get this extremely intense feeling of passion, pride, and joy that courses through my veins and a burning fire in my chest. I am not being metaphorical; I can literally feel the heat in my chest. Once I felt that, I knew what my calling was, and I knew the reason I was put on this Earth. As cheesy as that may sound, there was no denying the fire inside me. It was a defining moment for me, when I was finally able to admit to myself that I was living for something bigger than myself and I had the power to achieve that. I finally hooked my claw at the top of that bucket and started to slowly drag myself out.

Being honest with myself about my "Big Why" was liberating. This allowed something amazing to happen. My "Big Why" allowed me to push through all of the hardships, tragedies, and bad days with the bigger vision of my extraordinary life. Before this realization, when I chose to do the things that moved the needle closer to my "Big Why," it was a want. It was because I wanted to be successful, have money, and live a life of luxury. But afterward? After I discovered my "Big Why," these actions I took every day were no longer a want—it was a burning need. I had to make waves. Your "Big Why" should be so powerful that it is no longer a choice of whether you will pursue it or not. This is an integral part of *how* you get out of the crab bucket. Once you realize that your "Big Why" is no longer a choice but a necessity, and that you'll do everything in your power to achieve it, you'll have escaped the grasp of what is holding you back.

Now that you have done the work to discover your "Big Why," let's get this out on paper so you can refer back to it. This is what is going to propel you forward as things get tough, and on the days when you can't possibly understand why you need to get up and hustle.

MY BIG WHY

_____

_____

_____

_____

_____

_____

_____

5

TRAINING THE SUBCONSCIOUS MIND

SOMEONE VERY IMPORTANT TO ME ONCE TOLD ME ABOUT THE theory of The Rider, The Elephant, and The Path. In this story, the Rider is our conscious, rational mind. The Rider plans, problem solves, and analyzes to choose life's directions. This is the goal setting process. The Elephant is our subconscious mind. Unlike the rational, conscious part of the brain that can create thoughts and ideas, the subconscious mind only receives information as the truth and acts upon it. The Path is the information that the Elephant receives and acts upon. If the Rider wants the Elephant to go a certain way, they must ensure there is a clear path for the Elephant to follow, one foot in front of the other, toward the destination. The Elephant isn't going to wonder what else is out there or doubt itself. It's just going to see what is in front of it (the Path) and act upon it. On the flip side of that, if the Rider doesn't provide a path for the Elephant, the Elephant will wander aimlessly. To sum it up, whatever your conscious mind thinks, decides, plans, and creates, your subconscious mind follows and acts upon.

Why is this such an important factor to getting out of the bucket? Well, the subconscious mind will receive information as fact, regardless of whether it is or not. If you are stuck in the bucket, wallowing in the filth of your bad habits and surrounded by toxic people and influences, your subconscious mind will perceive this as a fact. The subconscious doesn't ponder on what could be different or consider any possible change of your circumstances. Your subconscious is not rational; it receives information and acts. On the other side of that coin, if your subconscious mind is receiving good constructive habits, the power of your "Big Why," and the influences of people who build you up, it is going to act upon that information as a fact.

The first step to achieving this is to train your subconscious mind to believe these things *before* they actually happen. Whatever your subconscious mind believes is what will be. If your subconscious mind believes that you will be poor, you will be poor. If your subconscious mind believes you won't get the job, you won't get the job.

The powerful thing about this is that if your subconscious mind believes that you will conquer your comfort zone, you will get out. If your subconscious mind believes that you will be wealthy, *you will be wealthy.*

You have to believe! I first discovered the power of the subconscious mind through the book *You Were Born Rich* by Bob Proctor, and I delved deeper into it when reading Napoleon Hill's book *Think and Grow Rich.* Make it a priority to train your subconscious mind. Buy those books and learn from the experts.

After reading more into the subconscious mind, I was surprised by how seemingly simple this was. At first, I felt detached from my subconscious mind. Like I was on one side of the room and my subconscious mind was on the other, and I was trying to trick or deceive it into believing the things I wanted to change. However, you must fully accept that your subconscious mind and yourself are one. What I believed is what my subconscious mind believed. If I truly, with all of my being, believed that I would one day be wealthy, my subconscious mind would believe that, and so it would be.

Bob Proctor wrote down his huge, seemingly unimaginable, impossible goal onto a notecard. He got specific with what he wanted and when he wanted it. He carried this notecard with him everywhere and looked at it multiple times throughout his day, reaffirming to his subconscious mind that he *will* achieve this goal.

One of the most significant examples of this is when the actor Jim Carrey wrote himself a check for $10 million in 1985. He dated it for ten years in the future and labeled it as "acting services rendered." He kept this check in his wallet for the following decade and looked at it every single day. In November of 1995, he was cast in the movie *Dumb and Dumber* with a salary of $10 million. The subconscious mind is a powerful thing. It received this information and acted upon it as truth.

Since it might not always be sensible to carry around a notecard, or a check for $10 million, here is a revised edition for the twenty-first century. In this day and age, almost every single person owns a smartphone. Go into your "reminders" app and create your notecard.

You should already know what the goal is—your "Big Why"—but I want you to get specific with when you want it by. Remember, the subconscious mind receives information as fact, so we want to be as specific as possible. Once you create the reminder, set the notifications to remind you at *least* twice a day, once in the morning when you wake up and once in the evening before you go to bed. This is the bare minimum. For my "notecard" I have my reminder set on my home screen. This way, anytime I pick up my phone to unlock it, I am seeing the reminder of my specific goal, and my subconscious mind is receiving this information as a fact and acting upon it.

Whether your "notecard" is on your smartphone or in the literal sense, just create it, and make a commitment to yourself, and to me, that you will look at this note card at *least* twice a day and provide the information to your subconscious mind. Now that your subconscious mind believes it to be true, it's time to take action (more on that later).

Once your notecard is created, screenshot it or take a picture and post it on social media. Tag me @projectbadassbook and use the hashtag #projectbadassbook. Commit to it! I will see your commitment, so don't let me down.

Now that you have written it on paper in this book, and included it on your "notecard," physically or digitally, your subconscious mind is reading it. I want you to take it a step further and affirm it to your subconscious brain by speaking it out loud. Whatever information the subconscious receives, it believes.

This "Big Why" is what is going to help you craft your roadmap to your extraordinary life later on. Your subconscious mind believes, so now it's time to take the necessary actions.

6

FIRE & HIRE ACCORDINGLY

I'VE MENTIONED IT BEFORE, WHEN IT COMES TO GETTING OUT, AND more importantly staying out, of the crab bucket, who you surround yourself with is of the utmost importance. I'm sure you have all heard the saying that we are made up of the five people we surround ourselves with most. It's no secret that the people around us have an impact on our health, our mindset, our habits, and our goals. If you are surrounded by five addicts, you will be the sixth. If you are surrounded by five millionaires, you will be the sixth. Yet it seems that we have a hard time firing those who do not serve us and hiring the people who do. It may seem harsh, but if you are surrounding yourself with people who display signs of being in the bucket without any desire to change it, they are the wrong people to be associating with.

It is essential to surround yourself with people who will help you get out and stay out of the bucket. Finding people and developing the relationship with the ones who are living the lifestyle you are and achieving the goals you want to achieve will only be beneficial to your success. Your friends and family greatly influence the choices you make, so surround yourself with people who will help you make decisions that serve your "Big Why." I also think it's important to have people in your life that are striving to be better yet are "lower on the ladder" than you, as this gives you the opportunity to mentor someone else to their extraordinary life.

When it comes to hiring and firing the people in your life, it is important to remember that you have full control of your environment and full control of your actions. I am the first to admit that choosing who stays in your life is not always the easiest thing to do. In fact, it's even harder because the people you are firing are often close friends or family members. I have had to fire friends, family members, and coworkers from my life because you can screw up your entire path by surrounding yourself with people who are stuck in the bucket.

In my case, I had to completely remove my biological father from my life. To this day, that man is so far down in his bucket with no realization and no intention of getting out that being in contact with him would ensure that I would be right down at the bottom with him. When I was sixteen, I found out about my birth dad. In fact, for the first sixteen years of my life, I fully and completely believed that my adoptive dad was my birth dad. I had no reason to think otherwise, and it wasn't until I saw a text message that wasn't meant for my eyes that my world was turned upside down. In one sentence, what I thought of as the truth was completely wrong. I met my biological father shortly after and strived to have a relationship with him. Unfortunately, I started to see the signs. So I made the cut, and he is no longer one of the people who have any influence on me whatsoever. At the age of sixteen, this was heartbreaking to me because I couldn't quite understand why my biological father decided to abandon me before I was born. I also couldn't understand why my heart broke so much when I decided to make the cut. I have experienced other necessary heartbreaking choices throughout my life, and I realize that the choices you make to get out of the crab bucket aren't easy, and they usually hurt like hell too.

It's time to seriously reflect on the relationships you hold and determine if they make the cut. Do they help you grow or are they holding you back? Do they raise your standards and help you become a better person or are they stuck in the bucket with no intention of getting out? If it's the latter, make the cut.

7

DEVELOPING A GROWTH MINDSET

YOU HAVE DONE THE WORK TO PREPARE YOURSELF FOR YOUR extraordinary life by discovering what is holding you back and clarifying what will propel you forward. The next step is to take action to create your extraordinary life. The first part of this process is to develop a growth mindset, which will allow you to seek the knowledge and information to continuously better yourself. When I made it a goal to develop a growth mindset, it allowed me to think big and focus on the skills I needed to reach my full potential. I learned to consume as much information as I could, read more books, listen to more podcasts, and invest in training and education.

Not long before I started writing this book, I invested $16,000 into a twelve-month coaching program that took me to Miami four times to train with the best in business and real estate investing. For me, that was a *lot* of money. But I knew that what I invested in myself in time and money I would see returned in far greater amounts.

Having a growth mindset is critical to your extraordinary path. Why? Because *everything* you want is on the other side of your comfort zone. Get uncomfortable by pushing yourself to limits far greater than you ever thought were possible. Get uncomfortable by taking a risk and investing in yourself and your "Big Why." This is what the successful are doing. They invest in themselves because they have embraced the fact that they are lifelong learners and will *always* continue to learn and grow, to better themselves. The exciting thing about growth is there is no ceiling, no cap. You can always better yourself, there is no one and nothing that can keep you from reaching your wildest dreams.

Take it from someone who was not familiar with the growth mindset. Growing up as a kid, I can understand the negative feeling you have when thinking about investing time and money in yourself. I remember asking myself, "Isn't that selfish?" and saying, "That's too big of a risk." Other thoughts ran through my head: "I don't have the skill set to make that money back." "It'll just be a waste." "It feels like an unnecessary expense." There is a quote that says, "If you don't take risks, you will always work for someone who does." Undoubtedly, I was meant to be an entrepreneur. I knew I had to take risks, or I'd risk not achieving my dreams. I will make it happen, whatever it takes. And to start, I had to change my mindset, from a fixed to a growth mindset. Let's define it.

FIXED MINDSET TRAITS

- Avoids Challenges
- Gives Up Easily
- Is Threatened by Other People's Success
- Ignores or Resents Feedback and Constructive Criticism
- Has No Desire to Learn
- Believes That Effort Is Fruitless
- Never Improves Skills

GROWTH MINDSET TRAITS

- Embraces Challenges and Believes They Are Opportunities
- Perseveres through Failures and Challenges
- Accepts Feedback and Constructive Criticism
- Has a Strong Desire to Learn
- Believes Effort Is the Path to Mastery
- Finds Other's Successes Inspiring

Elon Musk sold PayPal for $180 million. After the sale, he invested all of his money into five different companies. After investing, he had nothing and had to borrow money for rent. He believed in his personal and business growth so passionately that he was willing to sleep on the street or borrow rent money after making $180 million from PayPal in order to make his dreams happen. That was in 2002. In early 2021, he became one of the richest people on the planet. Currently his net worth is $185 billion. I can only imagine what he will be worth when you are reading this book.

Stephen Curry said, "Success is not an accident, success is a choice." Elon Musk chose to risk everything and put millions of dollars on the line in order to make his dream a reality. Before I shifted my mindset, I thought "self-help" books were a load of shit. I'll be honest with you, I didn't believe in them at all. I thought, "If it's meant to be, it'll be." Thinking back on it now, I can't believe I believed such bullshit. Take control! It'll be because *you* make it happen, no one else.

GRAB LIFE BY THE BALLS AND TAKE WHAT YOU WANT. NO ONE ELSE IS GOING TO DO IT FOR YOU.

Once I embraced the growth mindset, I saw the truth that had been yelling at my face for years. You, and only you, are 100 percent responsible for the growth of yourself and your success. Don't get comfortable, don't get stagnant, don't coast. Developing a growth mindset is a surefire way to make sure you don't live life on autopilot.

After developing a growth mindset, as cliché as it sounds, failure is no longer the thing I am most scared about—it's not growing. I am terrified, more than anything else in the world, that I will be in the exact same place I am today in a month, six months, or a year from now. I am terrified that I will find myself at the bottom of the same bucket that I am at today. After putting my growth mindset into action, I am able to think big. And by that, I mean really *big*. Having the mindset of being able to achieve anything I set my mind to and having the tactics to actually make that happen for myself was life changing. My subconscious mind believes that I will do extraordinary things and my growth mindset gives me the tools to do so.

The coolest thing about the growth mindset is that every piece of information we need to know or crave to know is at our fingertips. You no longer have to attend four-plus years of college and dump thousands of dollars into a secondary education in order to learn the skills to make money. After attending three semesters of business school, I still had zero clue how to start and run my own business, let alone be successful at it. I dropped out and got connected with the right people. I started to develop the mindset and seek out the information I needed to run a successful business. Suddenly the pathway of how I was going to succeed became clearer.

Not taking your growth into your own hands is the equivalent to standing at the bottom of the bucket, looking up at the light, but not doing a damn thing about it. You are holding your hands up, shrugging your shoulders and saying, "Oh well, it'll happen if it's supposed to happen." What a shame. There is so much wasted potential by those who do that!

The unfortunate truth is that the majority of people are living out this complacent scenario every single day. Sadly, they don't even realize they are doing it, because their brains were wired to complacency from the very beginning. That's total bullshit! We were *not* put on this Earth to just grow up, go to work, pay bills, and then die. There is nothing different between you and I, or anyone else who has gotten out of the bucket—with one exception. The only difference is that we were shown the truth of how to get out of the crab bucket and acted upon it. If you want something, go get it. It's completely up to you. Accept that everything you do and the things that you want to achieve are completely in your control. Never stop growing. It's time to act upon your dreams.

I wanted to give you some tactical ways to start shifting to a growth mindset and provide content you can consume to continue your growth journey. For me, books are one of the most important keys to growth. Here are some of my favorites:

1. *Be Obsessed or Be Average*, Grant Cardone
2. *Rich Dad Poor Dad*, Robert Kiyosaki
3. *Think and Grow Rich*, Napoleon Hill
4. *I Was Born Rich*, Bob Proctor
5. *Bluefishing*, Steve Sims
6. *The Go Giver*, Bob Burg
7. *The 10X Rule*, Grant Cardone
8. *Secrets of the Millionaire Mind*, T. Harv Eker
9. *The Science of Getting Rich*, Wallace D. Wattles
10. *15 Invaluable Laws to Growth*, John C. Maxwell
11. *Atomic Habits*, James Clear
12. *How to Be a Power Connector*, Judy Robinett

Consume, consume, consume! When I first started my growth journey, I purchased a small journal and wrote down everything that stood out to me when consuming content, whether it was from a book, seminar, or podcast. Then

I would start implementing ideas, one at a time. It didn't matter how quickly or slowly I was doing it. It mattered that I was actually doing it, and one small improvement at a time was pulling me closer and closer to the top of the crab bucket. These authors will become your mentors. Surrounding yourself with mentors that embody a growth mindset is a great way to grow.

Start by seeking out those who are living the life you want to experience and are succeeding at the things you want to achieve. Success leaves clues. Pay attention and pick up the obvious clues that are left behind by the people who are leading the life you want to live. I guarantee that you know at *least* ten people you could reach out to right now and connect with. Write down ten people that you could contact today who could help you get closer to achieving your goals. These ten people are going to be the start of your "power base." You can provide value to them and they can give value to you. And from those ten, you can continue to grow your network.

MY POWER BASE

1. _____

   _____

2. _____

   _____

3. _____

   _____

4. _____

   _____

5. _____

   _____

6. _____

   _____

7. _____

   _____

8. _____

   _____

9. _____

   _____

10. _____

   _____

My recommendation is to reach out over a phone call. Here's an example of what you could say:

> "Hey John, it's Madison Reeves. I'm not sure if you remember me, but we met about a month ago at one of the Chamber events. My good friend Trevor introduced me to you! The reason for my call is that I am interested in taking you out for lunch next week to see what I can do to assist you. I would love to learn more about what you do and how you do it. Do you have availability Tuesday or Thursday of next week?"

Simple. Easy. If they say yes, fantastic! Take your notebook and write down every key piece of information you take away from them and start to implement it. However, these relationships are not a one-time thing, and they are definitely not a one-way street. Nurture the relationship, provide value, and build it. You will thank me later. The wealthy value connections and you will too. Dig deep during this lunch meeting. Figure out what *they* need and how *you* can help them. Don't forget the most important thing, ask your Top 10 who they know that you can add to your Power Base and meet with.

If they say no? That's fine too. Keep following up until they say yes. Once they see that you are committed to meeting them, they will eventually cave. Keep at it, stay consistent. As a business owner, if I had someone continue to follow up with me, relentlessly, I would take the meeting just to get them off my back.

Your next couple of weeks should be packed full of meetings with the top ten from your Power Base. Once that's finished, I guarantee you will have a notebook full of information to implement, podcasts to listen to, books to read, and mentors to follow. Start your growth journey, provide value wherever you can, and build these relationships. Remember: consume, consume, consume!

Achievers get *out* of the bucket because they take the necessary action to leave their comfort zone. Ultimately, you must begin this journey with the conscious and subconscious decision to get out. It is completely necessary. People are stuck in the bucket because of their mindset. In fact, if you don't master your mindset, the remaining strategies and tactics in the book are going to be useless. It all starts within.

THE ACHIEVERS SAW THEIR FUTURE BURNING SO BRIGHTLY AHEAD OF THEM AND HAD THE BURNING DESIRE TO MAKE THAT HAPPEN, AGAINST ALL ODDS.

It wouldn't be easy, it wouldn't be comfortable, and their brain would make them want to stay in their bucket. However, armed with their "Big Why," the achievers are willing to put it all on the line and take a risk for their extraordinary life.

Because society believes that getting out of the bucket is impossible, the majority are conditioned to believe this too. Once you can reach that growth mindset and see through the mask, you'll understand that it is a simple process to get out of the bucket. Don't get me wrong, it won't be easy. But it is a simple process to follow. Unfortunately for crabs, when more than one crab is in a bucket, none will ever get out. Fortunately for us, as human beings, there *is* a way to escape.

PART 3

GETTING OUT OF THE BUCKET

8

SACRIFICE NOW

YOUR "BIG WHY" IS GOING TO MOTIVATE YOU FORWARD AS WE move through the next part of the book and through the necessary work that will release you from what is holding you back. Keep in mind why you are doing this and keep a growth mindset. Now that you are able to recognize your bucket and what is keeping you there, it's time to eliminate the bad habits, the negative people around you, and the environments holding you back.

For an entire week, I want you to carry around this book and use the next couple of pages to write down every bad habit, every energy-sucking negative person around you, and every substandard environment holding you back. Write down anything in your life that doesn't contribute to your "Big Why."

MY BAD HABITS, NEGATIVE INFLUENCES & SUBSTANDARD ENVIRONMENTS

CHAPTER 8: SACRIFICE NOW

After writing your bad habits down in black and white, they are impossible to ignore. After completing this exercise for the first time, some of the items on my list felt restrictive. I had to prioritize going to bed at a certain time so I could wake up, take advantage of my morning, and show up as my best self. This was hard for me because I am typically a person who would stay up later, scrolling through social media and waking up late the next morning. I fought myself on changing because the restrictiveness felt uncomfortable—my comfort zone was being threatened. Staying up late scrolling through Facebook felt good, whereas prioritizing my sleep and morning routine felt uncomfortable. But I knew that in order to achieve my "Big Why" I would have to give up some of these things. You may be feeling the same way, but now is the time to sacrifice.

As I said, having all of these things written down on paper makes them impossible to ignore. This exercise wasn't meant to just make you uncomfortable looking at every bad habit laid out plainly. I want you to take it a step further and work on eliminating each of these bad habits, as this will move the needle closer to your extraordinary life. I don't expect you to wake up in the morning and suddenly be rid of these negative habits. Unfortunately, it doesn't work like that. There are multiple studies out there that talk about how long it takes to build or break a habit, but the amount of time that has worked well for me is sixty-six days.

The next step of this exercise is to review your list and pick the top habit you want to break in the next sixty-six days. Taking it a step further, not only are we going to work on breaking the habit, we are also going to work on building a healthy habit to take its place. Try breaking the habit of looking at your phone right before bed by creating a habit of putting it on the charger, in a separate room, at least forty-five minutes before you go to sleep. Choose a bad habit and a healthy habit you want to replace it with and commit to that plan for the next sixty-six days, minimum. Put an alarm on your phone to remind yourself or tell your spouse or roommate so they can help hold you accountable. I want you to commit to yourself and your subconscious mind that you will dedicate the next sixty-six days to building this healthy habit to replace the negative one. What better way to do so than write it out here and now? Your subconscious mind will see this information and receive it as fact.

STARTING TODAY _____ (TODAY'S DATE)
I COMMIT TO BREAKING THE NEGATIVE HABIT OF

_____

BY BUILDING THE HEALTHY HABIT OF

_____

IN THE NEXT 66 DAYS.

Start whittling your list down, replacing one bad habit with one healthy habit at a time. Keep a growth mindset, with a clear vision of your "Big Why" in the forefront—your self-awareness will grow.

As much as we all want the life of luxury, sitting by the poolside, drinking a cocktail while someone else runs your business and you collect a check from it—trust me, that's where I want to be—that's not how success works. Success takes dedication, hard work, and sacrifice. For the first handful of years, you *will* be working eighty-plus hours a week, you *will* be missing the parties, the holidays, the days off. If you put the hours in, if you stick consistently with the work, you *will* see lasting success. If you stay consistent and dedicated to eliminating your bad habits, you will see lasting success.

Behind every successful person is a lot of unsuccessful years and a lot of sacrifices made. One of my favorite quotes is, "Sacrifice now so you may live a life most people only dream of." If you were willing to put your head down and disappear for a while, can you imagine what your life would look like in six months, one year, or five years from now?

There are plenty of temptations that come up in my daily life. Choosing Netflix over reading, eating out over cooking, going to the party over staying home to build my business. I am not different from anyone else—I am still tempted. I always ask myself a series of questions:

- "Am I craving this for short-term pleasure or long-term gain?"
- "Is the decision I am making now moving the needle toward my "Big Why"?"
- "Am I repeating bad habits because I am stuck in the bucket or is this decision contributing to my extraordinary life?"

If you can recognize that distinction and choose the long-term gain, you'll progress more than ever before. Ask yourself these three questions any time you want to skip the gym or push snooze one more time.

I challenge you to relish the path that gets you to the longer-term gain. Enjoy the tedious, consistent and even boring work, knowing this is what moves you closer to your extraordinary life. I am the girl who worked on Thanksgiving, Christmas Eve and New Year's Day. I am the girl who chooses to put my head down and grind on my goals every single day. I am the first one to show up and the last one to leave. With this work ethic, I have heard the same thing my entire life: "Why don't you slow down and enjoy life a little?" What they don't understand is that the more I sacrifice now, the larger I can live five and ten years from now. It's because I am out of the crab bucket that I am able to see this perspective from a broader view. Those still stuck in their comfort zone look at the sacrifices as a negative thing, where I think of them as a positive, necessary sacrifice. It's not even a choice. Do I want to achieve an extraordinary life? Yes! Great, then I will sacrifice.

9

LEADERS RISE ABOVE

SO, HOW DID I GET OUT OF THE BUCKET? THERE ARE A HANDFUL OF distinct, memorable moments in my life that contributed to recognizing the signs of my crab buckets and making small steps to getting out. If I think back to all of the life-changing and pivotal moments in my life, it took harsh real-life mistakes to put things into perspective. I had a breaking point that finally forced me over the edge of the bucket, gasping for air and craving something new.

That moment was watching my marriage fail. I was married at a very young age, and looking back on it now, even though we loved and cared for each other, we got married too young, and we married the wrong people. It was a bucket that I fell feet over face into. It was almost as if I was flying above the whole thing, and I could see exactly what was going to happen before it did. Knowing that it was failing and how it would play out didn't make it easier. Especially when I was faced with a pivotal moment, looking down a fork in the road. I could go right and stay in the bucket. I could stay with my husband, we could have babies and buy a somewhat decent house, and I could try to live a satisfied and content life. That was the route expected of me. Despite the fact that I knew with every fiber of my being that this path was wrong for me, I could have very easily stayed stuck at the bottom of this bucket to preserve the marriage vows I had once made and to stay comfortable and safe. My environment had conditioned me to take the "less risky" option. I would be generally happy, not fulfilled, but happy enough. But I would always be thinking about that extraordinary life I didn't take. I would always be wondering whether I made the right decision, a part of me always pulling the opposite direction, away from my husband and children. That wouldn't be fair to them, and it certainly wasn't fair to me.

My other option was to go left and take the path that was unexpected and risky. I could leave my husband and do the thing that terrified me. I could choose my career over my marriage. I could choose myself over my husband. I could choose my extraordinary life over any future that we had together and any vows that we had committed to.

Unfortunately, this wasn't a situation where I could have both. Staying with my husband would have kept me in the bucket that I was already in, no longer able to crawl my way out. He didn't share the same vision of the extraordinary life as I did. It was scary as hell to even consider because I had no idea where I would end up. I was out of my comfort zone. I could end up broke, a failure in my business, homeless. I could end up alone and divorced at nineteen. These were all possible consequences I faced when looking down this path. Honestly, it scared the shit out of me. It took me almost six months to make this pivotal decision, because I was terrified of what life outside of the bucket would look like. But I knew it would get me out of my comfort zone and open a path that I had always dreamed about.

I decided to make a left turn, to take that risk. I made the choice to leave my husband, to leave the content life full of weekend soccer games, a nine-to-five job, and TV on the weeknights. With one decision, I was divorced at nineteen, I was homeless, and I was alone. I wanted none of those things. It was uncomfortable, painful, and embarrassing as hell. I was fumbling down this dark and potentially destructive path. I had no idea what was going to happen to me or where I was going to land. But all of those things were what I had to endure to get out of the bucket and become the person I was meant to be.

I have made *massive* mistakes, and I have experienced tragedy. These pivotal moments have all played a critical role in creating the person I am today, and they have *all* played a role in getting me out of the bucket. I do believe that success breeds from a certain amount of tragedy. Almost every successful person I look up to started from nothing and has experienced horrible, terrible things. Every time I have experienced a tragedy, made a mistake, or overcame a hurdle, it has been a pivotal moment for me, pulling myself, one experience at a time, out of what is comfortable, safe, and recognizable. That was hard to realize in the moment. It was like driving through a pitch-black tunnel I couldn't see the end of. These experiences showed me who I didn't want to be and the life I didn't want to lead. They pushed me to surround myself with the people, knowledge and mindset of who I *do* want to be and the life I *do* want to lead.

Before I could get out of the crab bucket, I had to fully accept my experiences, despite feeling cheated out of a normal childhood and healthy relationships. I had to accept the tragedy and hardships I have faced, regardless of how painful it is. I accepted the sacrifices I have already made to get where I currently am, and the sacrifices I will have to make to get where I want to be. I used to feel cheated and defeated by the things I had to experience while growing up. I felt jealous that I didn't have the same lifestyle as other people and embarrassed of the hardships I went through. Because of this, I waited an entire year before telling a single soul about my sexual assault. I waited the better part of a month before sharing that I knew about my birth dad. My own mother didn't know I was getting divorced until I was homeless and had nowhere to go. I was embarrassed by these things and was uncomfortable accepting that these experiences would help me grow into a stronger, more successful human being. Waiting to accept and call out for help slowed down the healing process. Whatever experiences you have endured, whatever tragedies you have faced, rise above and embrace that these moments made you stronger and reinforced that extraordinary life you are working toward. Use these experiences as a stepping-stone to get closer to your "Big Why."

After getting out of the bucket, recognizing the path that got me here, and knowing how to stay out of the bucket, I can honestly say that I have *never* felt more like myself. That is the most liberating feeling. All of these small, seemingly insignificant things changed my life and myself in a very pivotal way.

I think it is important to discuss what it looks like to stay out of the bucket. Much like a recovering addict, it's important that you have the tools to not relapse. Our brains still function the same way: the bottom of the bucket still makes us feel comfortable. There will most definitely be days where you will feel like falling back into that bucket. You will have to train yourself to continuously strive for the uncomfortable. Developing the correct mindset, surrounding yourself with those on the same journey as you, and creating a healthy environment will certainly help keep you from relapsing into what is comfortable. However, you can't do this on your own. As the famous quote says, "if you want to go fast, go alone. If you want to go far, go together." You *need* the right people, the right mindset, and the right environment to ensure that you won't relapse and fall back into comfortability.

Your "Big Why" should be more desirable than the bottom of your crab bucket. Your need for an extraordinary life should be so bright and so strong that you crave it more than relapsing to the bad habits and comfort zone that feels so good. It should be so strong that you rise above the bad habits, negative environments, and toxic people. With the right tools, you can pull yourself out of your bucket and see the light. Keep pushing, keep growing, keep getting uncomfortable. It's a bright world out there—and it's so damn exciting that the only thing standing between yourself and your full potential is you, and now you have the tools to achieve it.

PART 4

RUNNING TOWARD YOUR EXTRAORDINARY LIFE

10

CAST YOUR VISION

NOW THAT YOU CAN RECOGNIZE EXACTLY WHAT IS HOLDING YOU back, have done the work to push yourself forward, and discovered your "Big Why," it's time to start on the pathway toward the extraordinary. I want to deliver on my promise and give you the tools, resources, and first steps forward in order to achieve that extraordinary life. I am a big believer in true, actionable, forward-moving steps. If you've made it this far, I know you have it in you to fulfill that extraordinary life that you can't stop thinking about.

Before we create your *Roadmap* to your extraordinary life, let's start by envisioning exactly what your extraordinary life looks like. We did this on a smaller scale when discovering your "Big Why," but I want to take it a step forward and really get into the nitty-gritty details of what this life will look like for you.

We are going to do a manifesting exercise that will paint a picture of exactly what you want out of your extraordinary life. Start by reviewing the following questions. Answering these will paint a picture of your extraordinary life.

- Where will you be living?
- What does your house look like?
- What is your career?
- What does a typical day look like for you?
- What does a typical weekend look like for you?
- Who will you be surrounded by?
- What does your bank account look like?
- When exactly will you achieve this?
- What activities do you do every single day to serve your "Big Why"?

With these questions in mind, find a quick place to sit by yourself for the next several minutes. Set the book open in front of you and close your eyes. As you answer each one of these questions, and any others they pop up as you are doing this exercise, start to paint a picture in your subconscious mind, to visualize exactly what your extraordinary life looks like.

This picture of your extraordinary life should fulfill you in every way possible: your career, your money, your relationships, your spirituality, and your health. You should be so fiercely passionate about everything you're doing that you can't wait to wake up every day and build your empire. Doing this exercise and vividly painting this picture announces what you want and when to your subconscious mind. Your subconscious mind will then act on this information.

You will likely gain an unprecedented amount of clarity from completing this exercise. For me, the feeling was intense because there was no more guessing and no more hiding. By engaging my subconscious mind, I started to believe that this extraordinary life was already mine. That set my soul on fire. I truly believed that I had the power to get anything I wanted, and that everything I needed to achieve success came from within myself. I hope it does the same for you.

"I SURVIVED BECAUSE THE FIRE INSIDE ME BURNED BRIGHTER THAN THE FIRE AROUND ME."
–JOSHUA GRAHAM

This exercise can be helpful to revisit again and again. It can be helpful to remember this vision on the hard days, when you face challenges or rejection. Feel free to come back to these exercises when you need a reminder of why you do what you do.

Now that you have completed this exercise, ask yourself . . .

- "Is your why BIG enough?"
- "Is your vision of your extraordinary life big enough to propel you through all of this painful change?"

I can guarantee you that if my vision and my "Big Why" were too small, there is absolutely no way I would have survived getting out of the bucket and starting this journey. When everything and everyone in my life was changing, the only thing that kept my head above water was the vision of my extraordinary life. Without that vision, I would have been swept beneath the waves. And knowing that you have this grand vision for yourself is not always enough to tread the dark waters. You'll often have to revisit these pages and remind yourself of your vision and exactly what you are fighting for.

I have always been a dreamer. I have always had a big vision for myself and felt like I could leave a mark on this world. However, growing up, I didn't have the right direction, clear instruction, or correct support system to tactically push myself forward. I didn't have any of the necessary tools to take that step forward until I started my journey out of the crab bucket. I often like to think of myself in two versions. *Madison Before* I got out of the bucket and started my journey toward an extraordinary life, and *Madison After*.

In fact, those two versions of myself are so drastically different that I hardly recognize who I was before. I am not the only one who can't recognize *Madison Before*, either. When I got really clear on what my vision of my extraordinary life looked like, my entire being transformed in front of my eyes and the eyes of my friends and family. And as we talked about before, when you get out of your comfort zone and change your life, those who are around you often get angry, upset, or uncomfortable. They might start to use the phrases like "You've changed," "I miss how you used to be," or "I liked you better before." I heard all of these things and many others from those who were closest to me—my mother and step-father, family members, even my two best friends who were a part of my life for the better part of a decade. The version of me after made those around me uncomfortable. As much as it sucked, it was a necessary part of the growth journey. This journey of growth *should* transform you for the better and so drastically that those around you won't recognize you anymore.

Even though it's hard for those people in my life to admit it out loud, their feelings about me aren't necessarily directed toward me. More often than not, they are reflecting on what they are feeling inside, just like the crabs in the bucket. The thing is, if your vision is powerful enough and the desire for your extraordinary life is bright enough, these lost or changed relationships won't matter. Those who truly love and care for you will adapt with your transformation to your better self. And the relationships that don't adapt will simply dissolve to make room for the relationships that will support you in the journey toward your extraordinary life.

I am very thankful that my mother and step-father adapted to my transformation. It wasn't easy on them, and I know that. But we got through the difficult times and they now understand that I am working toward something bigger than myself. But I also had relationships in my life that weren't strong enough to withstand that drastic transformation. Some of my closest friendships and even my marriage didn't hold strong against the winds of my transformation. I don't blame anyone for that either. It's really not their fault after all. My husband was married to someone (*Madison Before*) who no longer existed, and my best friends grew a friendship with someone (*Madison Before*) who was no longer around. *Madison After* is different, and that's just not what they signed up for, and that's okay.

Madison Before was quiet, shy, soft-spoken, naïve, and too often used as a doormat for others to walk over. Most of my relationships were with older people. So *Madison Before* assumed she should follow their lead, their advice, and their thoughts of what her life direction should be, because they were older, wiser, and more experienced. I let this mindset guide my life—my decisions often reflected what other people wanted me to do.

Madison After is the complete opposite. Now, I am loud and outspoken. I take up space. I voice my thoughts and opinions even if the people around me are older, more successful, or more experienced. I follow my gut and intuition. I set standards for how I treat myself and others, and I expect those standards to be reciprocated in how others treat me. For the crabs still stuck in a bucket, *Madison After* is hard to swallow. The person I am now might not be as likeable or easy to get along with because I don't allow others to pull me back down into the bucket.

During your journey toward your extraordinary life, soak up every experience and be at peace with the life that you live *today*, knowing that each decision you make is helping you build your extraordinary life. Take note from the Keller Williams BOLD Law: "Be, Do, Achieve." First, I will be where I am. Second, I will do the necessary action that, third, results in my achievement. It's a careful balancing of "being" while also "dreaming" of that extraordinary life, and acting to achieve that vision as quickly as possible.

It starts with your mindset and the commitment to seeking your extraordinary life. Start today and don't let anything get in your way. Elon Musk said, "Stop being patient and start asking yourself, how do I accomplish my five-year plan in six months? You'll probably fail, but you'll be a lot farther along than the person who simply accepted that it would take five years." The journey toward an extraordinary life is not for the fainthearted. It's going to take grit and strength to keep yourself out of the crab bucket, and it's going to take massive action to reach your extraordinary life. With a powerful vision and a rock-solid mindset, there's absolutely nothing in this life that can stop you.

John Green uses the quote "I go to seek a Great Perhaps," the last words of the famous poet Francois Rebelias, in his book *Looking for Alaska*. In this book, John Green writes, "I don't want to wait until I die to start seeking the Great Perhaps." I want you to start seeking your Great Perhaps, your extraordinary life, your wildest dreams, *today*.

11

CREATE YOUR BLUEPRINT

THE NEXT STEP IN YOUR JOURNEY TOWARD YOUR EXTRAORDINARY
life is creating your Roadmap: the plan of exactly what it will
take to get you to your goals. This is going to take out all the
guesswork, by putting your extraordinary life down on paper
and reverse engineering it to create small actionable steps on
how to achieve it.

But before I give you the steps to creating your Roadmap,
I feel as if it's only fair to warn you about your extraordinary
life. You must be absolutely, positively ready for this extraordinary life and everything—good, bad, and ugly—that comes
with it. Because there is a lot of the bad and ugly. But the good
should be good enough to outweigh the negative. As we've
discussed before, though, this is not for the faint of heart. So
here it is . . .

THE WARNING ABOUT YOUR EXTRAORDINARY LIFE

1. **YOU WILL BECOME UNRECOGNIZABLE TO YOURSELF.** The transformation you're about to undertake is a powerful one, and despite it being positive, you will most likely become unrecognizable to yourself. When I look in the mirror, I no longer recognize myself from the person I was a year ago.

2. **YOU WILL BECOME UNRECOGNIZABLE TO THOSE AROUND YOU.** When you start to transform, others will see you differently. This could cause your relationships to crumble.

3. **YOU WILL HAVE A LOW TOLERANCE OF OTHERS TREATING YOU NEGATIVELY.** You will start to understand how other people can affect you (positively or negatively), and you may reassess who is allowed in your life and how they treat you. For me, it doesn't matter if you're blood, or if we've known each other for many years. If you treat me poorly and if you're hindering me from my extraordinary life, I will simply walk away.

4. **YOU WILL RELY LESS ON THOSE AROUND YOU AND RELY MORE ON YOURSELF.** Your pathway toward an extraordinary life will create a stronger, more independent you through the sheer challenges you will need to overcome. The people around you that like your dependence will start to fade away, because you no longer need them.

5. **YOUR OPINION AND PERCEPTION ON TOPICS MAY START TO SHIFT.** Through this journey you will be consuming books,

podcasts, and the thoughts of other people that have the same goals as you. You may start to see your preconceived notions of many topics shift.

6. **YOU WILL HAVE DAYS WHERE THE SMALL VOICE IN THE BACK OF YOUR HEAD WON'T SHUT UP ABOUT QUITTING AND DOING IT THE EASY WAY.** Hearing this is normal, it's expected. The path we have chosen is not the easy way. Just don't let this tiny voice pull you back down into what is comfortable and familiar.

7. **YOU WILL EXPERIENCE CHALLENGES GREATER THAN YOU WOULD HAVE EVER EXPECTED.** Inevitably, up to this point, you are sure to have experienced tragedies, same as me. Our path toward our extraordinary lives is harder than you can imagine. There is so much self-doubt, second guessing, wishful thinking, and wanting to take the easy way out. The things that happened to me before were external. But the challenges of working toward your extraordinary life are internal. They are completely caused by you and your mindset. The forward trajectory of your life is up to you and 100 percent influenced by your decisions.

8. **YOU WILL EXPERIENCE SETBACKS WHILE FOLLOWING YOUR ROADMAP.** As much as I hope that the following information will prepare your blueprint in the best way possible, I understand that there *are* going to be setbacks while following this pathway. It's not even a question of if, but of what and when. Going into this journey with the mindset that you are going to have to overcome hurdles and push through these setbacks will set you up for success. This journey is not going to be all rainbows and sunshine.

CREATING YOUR ROADMAP

A few key things to remember before you start to create your Roadmap:

1. Make sure you are creating SMART goals. As you write out your main objective, three priorities and five actions items, ask yourself these following questions

    a. "Is this goal **specific**?"

    b. "Is this goal **measurable**?" (a.k.a., at any given time, can I see my progress from where I've started to where I have to go?)

    c. "Is this goal **attainable**?" (especially within the time period you have set for yourself)

    d. "Is this goal **relevant**?" (hint: your goal should not be a part of your Roadmap if it is not relevant to your main objective)

    e. "Is this goal **timely**?" (set yourself a time limit: month, year, date)

2. When you are creating your Roadmap, make sure to list your SMART goals in order of priority and importance to the overall goal. Your first priority should be completed before any of the other action items are done.

Because we will reverse engineer your "Big Why" into smaller, easy-to-digest, actionable steps, I want to start with a large, birds-eye view of your top three priorities for achieving your "Big Why." These Top 3 Priorities are the most important focus points. By completing these priorities, you are sure to achieve the "Big Why." This will take out the guesswork of *how* to get to your end result and focus your time and efforts on *what* needs to be done in order to get there. Identifying the three key priorities helps because it utilizes the 80/20 rule, or the Pareto Principle. The 80/20 rule essentially says that 80 percent of your consequences (or results) come from 20 percent of causes (or actions). When determining your Top 3 Priorities, you are choosing the 20 percent actions (three priorities) that will create 80 percent of your results (the "Big Why"). By doing this, you are getting rid of all the unnecessary things that may seem like they matter to the end result but aren't really moving the needle forward.

To clarify these Top 3 Priorities, ask yourself, "What are the three most important actions to achieve my Big Why?" What exactly do I need to do? Again, we are starting broad and then we will get really granular. These priorities should be subsections of your "Big Why," but they are still the main objectives to achieving your "Big Why." Let's determine them now . . .

EXAMPLES OF MY TOP 3 PRIORITIES

My Top 3 Priorities to achieve my "Big Why" are . . .

1.
2.
3.

Your second step to creating your Roadmap is to further break down your Top 3 Priorities into your 5 Benchmarks. By completing these 5 Benchmarks, you will achieve the Top 3 Priorities and, in turn, your "Big Why."

Each one of your Top 3 Priorities will have a list of 5 Benchmarks to achieve them. For example, one of my Top 3 Priorities was to "publish a book in 2021," so my 5 Benchmarks were as follows:

1. Write a Rough Draft Manuscript
2. Find a Publisher
3. Start Building an Audience on Social Media
4. Spread the Word through Podcasts and Other PR
5. Edit and Publish

As you can see, each one of these 5 Benchmarks directly contributes to the progress of my Priority. Now it's your turn. Take a look at each of your Top 3 Priorities and determine what the 5 Benchmarks are for each.

1ST PRIORITY

_____

_____

BENCHMARK 1: _____

_____

BENCHMARK 2: _____

_____

BENCHMARK 3: _____

_____

BENCHMARK 4: _____

_____

BENCHMARK 5: _____

_____

2ND PRIORITY

_____

_____

BENCHMARK 1: _____

_____

BENCHMARK 2: _____

_____

BENCHMARK 3: _____

_____

BENCHMARK 4: _____

_____

BENCHMARK 5: _____

_____

3RD PRIORITY

_____

_____

BENCHMARK 1: _____

_____

BENCHMARK 2: _____

_____

BENCHMARK 3: _____

_____

BENCHMARK 4: _____

_____

BENCHMARK 5: _____

_____

At this point, you should be confident, without a shadow of a doubt, that by completing your 5 Benchmarks for each of the Top 3 Priorities, you will achieve the "Big Why."

When I asked a colleague of mine, who is a very successful real estate investor, how he reached his success, Scott said, "Daily goal setting with actionable items. Creating monthly benchmarks to my yearly goals. Focus."

Plain and simple, folks. Don't reinvent the wheel—do what has worked for successful people before you.

As you work through your Roadmap and inch closer and closer to your "Big Why"—and ultimately, your extraordinary life—it's important to use this tool for what it is: a Roadmap. Every action you take, every decision you have to make, refer back to your Roadmap to ensure that it fits into the 20 percent actions that are producing 80 percent of your results.

Feel free to visit www.projectbadassbook.com/resources for a copy of a blank Roadmap for your future use.

Even once you have crafted your Roadmap, I want you to remember that this is only one part of your journey. If you stopped right now and never took the second step, you wouldn't reach your destination. Sure, you might have this Roadmap, but if you don't do anything with it, you'll be right back into your crab bucket, just looking at the clear pathway to the life you desire.

The second step is to start taking action. By testing out your Roadmap, you'll find out which actions matter to the overall cause, and what actions are not necessary to take. Work smarter, not harder.

UTILIZING THE ACCOUNTABILITY TOOL

You might have asked yourself, "Now that I have my Roadmap, how exactly do I complete it?" That's where the Accountability Tool comes in.

This tool is going to set each of your Benchmarks onto a timeline, so that you can predict your outcome and track your progress. Through this tool you will determine the annual goals, monthly goals (that will work toward your annual goal) and weekly tasks (that will work toward your monthly goals). This is an accountability and goal-tracking tool that you can and should use on a daily, weekly, monthly, and yearly basis.

To get started on utilizing yours, we are going to have you handwrite your Accountability Tool in this book, but make sure to head over to www.projectbadassbook.com/resources to get your free Accountability Tool resource that it is editable and easy to use via a computer, smartphone or tablet.

To start, fill in your "yearly" goals with your 5 Benchmarks. Even though we spent the time breaking down your Top 3 Priorities into 5 Benchmarks, we are going to break them down even further. These yearly goals aren't typically changed, unless you come to realize one is no longer relevant to your "Big Why."

Next are your "monthly" goals. These items will and should change on a monthly basis. When creating your monthly goals, these should be the specific tasks you need to complete that month to be on track to your "yearly" goals. For each specific month, you'll need to determine which Benchmark to complete to reach the Top Priorities in the yearly goal section.

Lastly, your "weekly" goals. These items, of course, will change on a weekly basis. This is your to-do list and your action items. When creating your "weekly" goals, determine what action item needs to be completed that week in order to achieve your "monthly" goals.

Remember: set SMART goals (specific, measurable, attainable, relevant, timely). By breaking each goal down into bite-size chunks, you ensure that you won't miss any critical tasks because you are working backward with your end goal in sight. See how it takes the guessing out of it? No more wondering what needs to be done in order to hit your goals.

Before creating your own Accountability Tool, I wanted to discuss a few points to keep in mind while you are crafting it. These are common and easy mistakes that people often make when creating their Accountability Tool for the first time.

1. For your "yearly" goals—each annual goal should have a specific deadline: day, month, and year, if possible. Often, these annual goals are what you want to achieve within the twelve months, but you may want to achieve some goals before December 31.

2. For any number you put on your Accountability Tool (e.g., goals for income, sales, word count), make sure to include the "+" sign after it. This signals to your subconscious brain that the goal number you have set for yourself is just the base, not the ceiling.

   a. For example: "I will make $150,000+ in profit by December 31, 2021."

3. For "weekly" goals, make sure these are actions and tasks that you can control completing. It is easy to add an action item that seems relevant but is out of your direct control. If that happens, break it down even further: "What action can I actually *control* to achieve this item?"

Now that you have a guide on how to utilize the Accountability Tool, it's time to put it down on paper. Utilizing your Roadmap and the instructions above, write it out now.

IN THE YEAR OF _____ , MY "YEARLY" GOALS ARE

◆ _____

_____

_____

_____

◆ _____

_____

_____

_____

◆ _____

_____

_____

_____

_____

IN THE MONTH OF _____ , MY "MONTHLY" GOALS ARE

◆ _____

_____

_____

◆ _____

_____

◈

DURING THE WEEK OF _____ ,
MY "WEEKLY" GOALS ARE

◈

◈

◈

You should be looking at your Accountability Tool at least once a day, if not more. You have decided that these action items, checkpoints, and benchmarks are your 20 percent—the most important tasks that will get you to your goal. This is your to-do list, so look at it every day, keep it at the top of your mind, and check off each item as it is completed.

The next important step is to transfer your weekly goals into your timeblock on your calendar and/or planner. Remember, "If it's not on your calendar, it doesn't exist." So, because you determined that these tasks *are* what is important, they should earn an important spot on your calendar to ensure they get completed before anything else. Remember, these tasks are what move you closer and closer, every day, toward your extraordinary life.

As an example, if one of my "weekly" goals is to pay off $500 in credit card debt, I am going to use my timeblock on my calendar to determine exactly when I am going to sit down, pull out the budget, and transfer the payment from my bank account to the credit card company. I need fifteen minutes to complete this necessary task, so therefore, it deserves a fifteen-minute block somewhere in my calendar this week. This ensures this important task gets completed.

For each weekly goal, you must determine exactly when you are going to do it, to make sure it gets done. For each weekly goal, ask yourself the following questions to determine the appropriate time block on your calendar.

1. **"How long will this task take me to complete?"** This is the amount of time I will need to timeblock for this task on my calendar. If you're a newbie to timeblocks,

I would recommend adding a margin for error. So if you guess this task will take you 1 hour, timeblock 1 hour 15 minutes on your schedule until you learn exactly how long it will take.

2. **"Does this task need to be completed on/or before a certain day?"** If yes, make sure you timeblock it for before the deadline. If no, and the task isn't necessarily time sensitive, stick it into your timeblock where you have available space.

3. **"Do I need another person in order to complete this task?"** If so, get in touch with that person to schedule a time to meet with them or give them a deadline to complete their portion of the task.

4. **"Do I need to complete any prep work before doing this task?"** If the answer is yes, reverse engineer this task so that you can break down each piece of the prep work. Timeblock each of these tasks.

If you can follow these instructions, you will have a Roadmap to your extraordinary life and a calendar full of needle-moving tasks. This Roadmap may change as you cross goals off your list or determine that a goal was not as important as originally thought. Regardless of how your Roadmap changes throughout the journey, what is important is to not stray from your "Big Why." You'll have a solid and easy to follow framework to refer back to you. This is your textbook toward your extraordinary life.

12

MARCHING FORWARD, ROADMAP IN HAND

THERE ARE JUST A FEW THINGS LEFT THAT I WANT TO DISCUSS before sending you off, weapons in hand, into the battle toward an extraordinary life.

Now that we have determined the Roadmap to your extraordinary life, the last step I can give you is how to determine who the right people are to help you get there. We have talked about the necessity of firing the people in your life that no longer serve you, but now we're going to talk about finding the people necessary to push you to the extraordinary.

After I cast my vision, I realized that the lifestyle I had dreamed of was too far above my head to reach. I needed people in my life who could boost me up so I could reach farther. I needed people in my corner who could elevate me to that extraordinary life. I needed people in my circle who were already living that extraordinary life. And I did not have just one single person in my circle who was going to push me toward my full potential. I needed to determine who was going to be in my circle, or as Elena Cardone describes in her book *Build an Empire*, who was going to be in my "royal court."

When I went through the pivotal change from *Madison Before* to *Madison After*, I desperately needed a support system in my life that was going to push this new version of me to reach heights that *Madison Before* would have laughed at. I started building my circle when joining the real estate team that changed my life. I was suddenly surrounded by like-minded people who were talking about a grand life. They were talking about investing, building wealth, and overall becoming a better and a healthier person.

These people quickly became my closest friends and the people I wanted to build my empire with. They connected me with books and podcasts that expanded my knowledge and started sharing ideas that opened my mindset to things I never thought possible for myself. I started to deliver them value in return, and create strong relationships, to the point where they started to introduce me to their circle of people who were talking and practicing the same things I was.

As Judy Robinett says in her book *The Power Connector*, I was creating successful strategic relationships with people I wanted in my circle. These people were connecting me to their circle, and my network of strong, like-minded people grew larger and larger. We are going to discuss what to look out for when determining the people that will earn a spot in your circle. But the most important thing is becoming the person who attracts the people you want in your circle—other like-minded people who are on the journey toward their extraordinary life. Judy Robinett describes this perfectly in her book *How to be a Power Connector*: "People who create successful strategic relationships demonstrate ten essential character traits." They are "Authentic, Trustworthy, Respectful, Caring, Listening, Engaged, Patient, Intelligent, Sociable, and Connected."

We want to attract the right people to our circle, so it's important to demonstrate the traits that other like-minded people would be looking for. On the other side of the coin, it's also important to be aware of who you are letting into your circle. When choosing the people who have the privilege of being in your circle, ask yourself these questions to ensure they fit into the vision of your extraordinary life.

1. "Do they have the mindset of someone who is working toward their extraordinary life?"
2. "Do they have a victim mentality, or do they own up to their weakness and faults?"
3. "Are they able to add value to my life and journey, and am I able to add value to theirs?"
4. "Do they practice the lifestyle, habits and behaviors of someone who is working toward their extraordinary life or are their lifestyle, habits and behaviors hindering them from moving the needle forward?"

And the million-dollar question . . .

5. "Are they stuck in their comfort zone? And if they are, are they actively trying to get out or are they so oblivious they don't know they are stuck at the bottom?"

Analyze each important relationship in your life and ask yourself these questions to determine if these people earn a spot in your circle. Now, don't misunderstand me—I am not saying that you have to completely cut off the people in your life that don't fit these criteria. But maybe these people don't earn a spot inside your close circle. Visualize it like this:

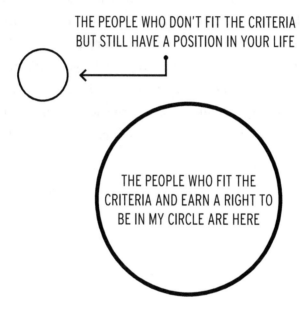

THE PEOPLE WHO DON'T FIT THE CRITERIA
BUT STILL HAVE A POSITION IN YOUR LIFE

THE PEOPLE WHO FIT THE
CRITERIA AND EARN A RIGHT TO
BE IN MY CIRCLE ARE HERE

Essentially, the people who are in your circle will be the ones who expand your network, share books and podcasts, and brainstorm topics that will expand your mindset. These people will deliver value to you and you to them. They are the ones you will confide in and ask advice from and the ones that will come to you when they need something. The 80/20 rule applies here as well. You are going to invest 80 percent of your time into your circle (the 20 percent).

In my life, the people in my circle are my mentors, coaches, and other business owners and entrepreneurs. We feed off of each other to expand our businesses and work toward that extraordinary life together. Because I have this circle of people in my life, I will go farther than I ever thought possible.

The people outside of my circle that I still have a relationship with are the ones who are not necessarily toxic to my "Big Why" but who are still stuck in the bucket. These are friends and family members that I grew up with who accept who I am now but haven't jumped on the bandwagon with me to reach their extraordinary life. By differentiating where these people stand, it simplifies who you should be pouring your time, energy, and value into. Relationships are everything!

13

THE 1% CLUB

AS WE NEAR THE END OF THIS BOOK, I WANT TO LEAVE YOU WITH one last piece of tactical advice before we wrap up the conclusion. Introducing the 1% Club. So, what is the 1% Club? Well, they are the people who exhibit specific behaviors, habits, actions, and mindsets to live their extraordinary lives. They completely and fully embody the lifestyle of a one percenter. For example, Elon Musk, Emily Weiss, Bill Gates, Mark Zuckerberg. I think we can all agree that these people are living their extraordinary lives, right? In fact, these four people have a collective net worth of billions of dollars. Like every other successful person, they have habits, behaviors, actions, and mindsets that allow them to achieve such high levels of success. They are living the lifestyle of a one percenter. I want to discuss a few of these highly productive routines to help you differentiate the routine of someone in the 1 percent and the routine of someone in the 99 percent.

The average person sleeps around 6.5 hours per day, works an average of 8.8 hours per weekday, and spends 4.5 hours doing leisure activities. Studies show that only 17 minutes of leisure time are spent exercising while 4.5 hours on weekdays are spent in front of the TV. So there you have it, folks. If you clock in less than 2.5 hours in front of the television, spend more than 15 minutes exercising, and spend more than 8.8 hours working toward your career or job, you are already leaps and bounds ahead of the average person. No wonder the 1% Club is so empty. Knowing how the average person spends their day, let's take a look at the extreme, almost laughable difference between that of an average person and that of someone who truly lives the lifestyle of a one percenter.

ELON MUSK'S MORNING ROUTINE[1]

With a usual bedtime of 1:00 a.m., Elon Musk wakes up at 7:00 a.m. He mentioned that 6–6.5 hours of sleep is his perfect amount of rest. He usually skips breakfast but grabs a coffee to save time. He attributes his morning shower to a source of great ideas. He spends time exercising, usually running on the treadmill or lifting weights. From there, he heads on to work and spends a majority of his time on SpaceX and Tesla each week, usually working 80+ hours in total.

---

1. See https://www.balancethegrind.com.au/daily-routines/elon-musk-daily-routine

MARK ZUCKERBERG'S MORNING ROUTINE[2]

Mark usually wakes up around 8:00 a.m., where he immediately checks on his businesses (as most CEOs do) and then hits the gym to get a good workout in. After, he eats breakfast and simply gets ready for the day. He doesn't waste time making small decisions, so we usually see him in the same attire: jeans and a T-shirt. He typically works 50–60 hours per week and focuses on spending quality time with family. He also challenges himself to read a new book every two weeks.

1. They all know and understand the value of sleep. It's true, in order to achieve your extraordinary life, it's important to work hard. But without the right amount of sleep for your body, you won't be showing up as your best self when it matters most. Determine a set time you go to bed and a set time you wake up. Be disciplined. Set your phone on "do not disturb" after you go to bed and follow this behavior.
2. They all spend time exercising. Health is wealth after all, and if you aren't taking care of yourself by exercising and eating right, you aren't going to show up the best for your extraordinary life.
3. They all understand the importance of time. It is our most valuable resource and should not be wasted.

2. See https://medium.com/@michaeljosephbonnell/a-look-inside-mark-zuckerbergs-morning-routine-6ef3ba8871ae

Mark Zuckerberg doesn't waste time making small decisions and emphasizes the priority of spending time with the people that matter the most

4. They all spend the majority of their day working in their career/business to move their needle forward toward their goals and extraordinary life. They are the epitome of working smarter, not harder, and utilizing the Pareto Principle.

Adopt the lifestyle of a one percenter. With those habits and routines, coupled with the Roadmap to your extraordinary life, you will be well on your way to your grand vision.

AT THIS POINT, YOU'VE BEEN GIVEN ALL THE TOOLS YOU NEED TO LIVE THE BADASS LIFE YOU DESIRE.

You've dug deep to figure out what is holding you back, and inevitably, what crab buckets you have been stuck in. You have looked at your bad habits and established a way to replace them with healthy, growth-mindset habits. And finally, you've created your Roadmap and the tools to hold yourself accountable. You aren't the person you were last year, or even sixty-six days ago.

I want you to know how proud of you I am for starting the journey toward your extraordinary life. I hope that this book will hold a special place on your bookshelf as you progress through the challenges and opportunities to come. I hope that you come back and check in a month, a quarter, a year, and five years from now to see the progress you've made and the badass life you have created for yourself.

This journey will not be easy. It's going to be hard, and you will face challenges and days where you will want nothing more than to give up and fall back into your comfort zone—back into the crab bucket that was holding you back from your full potential. When those days inevitably come, I hope that you pick this book up again and review the exercises you've completed and the tools in place that will help you stay away from your comfort zone—and to push you toward your next level.

Congratulations on the work you've done so far, and cheers to everything you will do in the future. Celebrate your success, fail forward through the challenges, and enjoy every minute of your journey to your own Project Badass.

ACKNOWLEDGMENTS

I OWE ALL THE SUCCESS I HAVE ACHIEVED THUS FAR, AND ALL that I will ever achieve, to the people listed below. Each and every one of you has changed my life and has helped me become the woman I am today.

Azul & Steve, from Authors Who Lead—Thank you for believing that I always had a book inside of me.

My publishing team—Thank you for your patience, kindness, and support on taking my jumbled thoughts and making them into something beautiful.

Abiah & Beth—Thank you for being the first to lay eyes on this manuscript.

Gillian, Roy & Rayna—Thank you for being the team that made sure I looked my best to be photographed for this book.

Mike—Thank you for bringing my vision and brand to life, and for providing me with such a clear voice so I have no issue speaking up and sharing my story.

Natalie—Thank you for encouraging me to write about the hard things in the book—for encouraging me to include the words that I may not have if not for your support.

ACKNOWLEDGMENTS

Jeff & Christina—Thank you for changing my life completely, for giving me the tools, support, and community to understand who I really am and chase after my wildest dreams.

With all the love in the world,

Madison Quinn

ABOUT THE AUTHOR

MADISON REEVES IS A SERIAL ENTREPRENEUR AND THE founder and CEO of both The Bridal Project and The Reeves Method, an event-planning company and coaching program, respectively. She is also an award-winning real estate agent, a recipient of the Top 100 Leaders in Real Estate award, and a top-producing sales team leader with Christians Team Inc. Madison is driven to help other entrepreneurs seek growth and take control of their results to accelerate their businesses and lives.

Madison grew up in a poor neighborhood in a small town and is determined to prove that anyone can fulfill their utmost potential, regardless of where they came from. After dropping out of college and getting fired from several jobs, she had seemingly no direction in life. It wasn't until Madison discovered entrepreneurship and creating a life she loved that she found her true calling and purpose in life. Now, she wants to share the liberation of an extraordinary life with others around her.

Madison spends her time mentoring other real estate sales agents with production coaching. She also focuses on expanding her real estate team to provide others with the same life-changing opportunity that was provided to her.

I WOULD APPRECIATE YOUR FEEDBACK ON WHAT
CHAPTERS HELPED YOU MOST AND WHAT YOU
WOULD LIKE TO SEE IN FUTURE BOOKS.

IF YOU ENJOYED THIS BOOK AND FOUND IT HELPFUL,
PLEASE LEAVE A **REVIEW** ON AMAZON.

VISIT ME AT

WWW.PROJECTBADASSBOOK.COM

WHERE YOU CAN SIGN UP FOR EMAIL UPDATES.

THANK YOU!

9 781954 801240